# BE A BETTER
# FOUNDATION STAGE TEACHER (NURSERY)

## by Judith Stevens

**Other titles in this series**

# BE A BETTER
# FOUNDATION STAGE TEACHER (NURSERY)

## by Judith Stevens

A division of MA Education Ltd

Teach Books Division, MA Education Ltd, St Jude's Church, Dulwich Road, London SE24 0PB

British Library Cataloguing-in-Publication Data
A catalogue record is available for this book

Printed in Malta by Gutenberg Press, Gudja Road, Tarxien PLA19, Malta

# CONTENTS

# INTRODUCTION

So you want to be a better foundation stage teacher in the nursery. What do you need to do to make that happen?

Well, you have already accomplished two huge steps forward. First, you have identified that you want to be a better teacher and, second, you have the enthusiasm to do something about it.

As foundation stage practitioners, we are in a very privileged position. We spend a large part of our days working and learning together with very special people. Children under five are the most vulnerable in our society and they deserve the support of interesting, interested adults who want to be with them. We need to be interested in the children as individuals, in what they are doing and in what their needs and current interests are. We also need to be interesting people who have things to talk about and share with children.

Working with young children can be one of the most rewarding careers in the world if you like being with young children, but one of the worst if you don't. Young children are active learners who are making sense of themselves and the world around them. This means that they are often noisy, messy, and demanding. It also means that they are challenging, exciting, funny and never, ever boring.

All nursery teachers must be good communicators and have the ability to be flexible and deal with the unexpected on a day-to-day basis. A positive, optimistic outlook and a very good sense of humour are prerequisites for nursery teaching. Although it is possible to enhance many characteristics through training or experience, these are personality traits which need to be within a person aspiring to be a better nursery teacher. As they say, 'you don't have to be superwoman or man to work here, but it does help!'

# BEING A BETTER FOUNDATION STAGE TEACHER

You will need expertise in three main areas:

1. The ability to apply knowledge.
2. Imagination and creativity.
3. Enthusiasm and effort.

## The ability to apply knowledge

You will need fully to understand:

- child development and how children learn
- the *Curriculum guidance for the foundation stage* (Qualifications and Curriculum Authority (QCA), 2000)
- areas of provision to support the six areas of learning
- effective assessment and planning
- current early years initiatives.

## Imagination and creativity

You will need to use imagination and creativity to:

- see the potential of seemingly mundane objects
- use basic resources in creative and exciting ways
- use books as starting points for stimulating experiences
- celebrate children's achievements and support their future learning through the environment
- be tuned in to children's needs and interests and be able to visualise experiences which will inspire individuals.

## Enthusiasm and effort

It will take enthusiasm and effort to:

- find the time and energy to source free and cheap objects
- develop inspirational role play areas
- go the extra step to ensure the learning environment is bright, interesting and exciting
- work with families and community members
- ensure children have easy access to appropriate resources which support them as successful, independent and autonomous learners.

This book aims to reinforce your understanding of the foundation stage and share practical ways to develop the learning environment. It will help you to plan for appropriate, interesting experiences which will make the time you spend with young children more stimulating and worthwhile for you all.

*When teaching in the nursery, make sure you say what you mean, and mean what you say. Then say it again, in a different way...*

*I spent that first day at school picking holes in paper, then went home in a smouldering temper.*

*'What's the matter Loll? Didn't he like it at school then?'*

*'They never gave me the present!'*

*'Present? What present?'*

*'They said they'd give me a present.'*

*'Well now, I'm sure they didn't.'*

*'They did! They said: "You're Laurie Lee, ain't you? Well just you sit there for the present." I sat there all day but I never got it. I ain't going back there again!'*

From *Cider with Rosie* by Laurie Lee

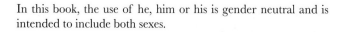

In this book, the use of he, him or his is gender neutral and is intended to include both sexes.

CHAPTER 1

# KEEPING ON TOP OF YOUR AREA

## INTRODUCTION

Being a better foundation stage teacher in the nursery requires an in-depth working knowledge of the *Curriculum guidance for the foundation stage* (QCA, 2000)\* and an understanding of current developments and issues in the early years. At present, these include:

- the 10-year strategy
- children's centres
- Key Elements of Effective Practice (KEEP) (Department for Education and Skills (DfES), 2005)
- self-evaluation
- seeing steps in children's learning
- development of a single quality framework.

This chapter seeks to outline what is important in keeping on top of the foundation stage and to identify where you can find out more, if you are interested.

## CURRICULUM GUIDANCE FOR THE FOUNDATION STAGE

The foundation stage was introduced as a distinct phase of education for children aged 3 to 5 in September 2000. *Curriculum guidance for the foundation stage* was distributed in May 2000 to all schools with reception or nursery classes, and to all early years settings receiving nursery education grant funding.

Subsequently, the Education Act 2002 extended the National Curriculum to include the foundation stage. The six areas of learning became statutory, and the Act also specified that there should be early learning goals for each of the areas. Following consultation, the early learning goals and the use of the *Curriculum guidance for the foundation stage* became statutory in March 2002. This clarified an earlier situation in which some reception class teachers felt unsure whether it was appropriate to be planning to the National Curriculum key stage 1 or the early learning goals.

The Act also established a single national assessment system for the foundation stage, replacing the numerous local baseline assessment schemes which had existed previously. The foundation stage profile was introduced in 2002\*. It has thirteen summary scales covering the six areas of learning, which need to be completed for each child receiving government funded education by the end of his or her time in the foundation stage. It needs to be made clear that the foundation stage profile is for use as a formative assessment tool during the whole of the reception year. It is not designed to be used in nursery classes. However, nursery practitioners do need to be aware of children's achievements in relation to *Curriculum guidance for the foundation stage* and to provide appropriate, accurate information about their progress when they transfer from nursery to reception classes (see *Chapter 2*)[†].

---

\* To receive a free copy of the *Curriculum guidance for the foundation stage*, reference QCA/03/1106, telephone QCA Publications 01787 884444

[†] To find out more about the foundation stage profile go to www.qca.org.uk

# Using *Curriculum guidance for the foundation stage*

When faced with the document, many practitioners make the error of turning straight to the six sections which outline the stepping stones and the early learning goals. This is sometimes seen as 'what' has to be taught. But the earlier sections of the guidance include vital information about 'how' the foundation stage should be implemented, and the fundamental principles which underpin it. These earlier sections include:

- aims for the foundation stage
- parents as partners
- principles for early years education
- putting the principles into practice
- meeting the diverse needs of children
- children with special educational needs and disabilities
- children with English as an additional language
- learning and teaching
- play.

## Principles for early years education

These principles are drawn from good and effective practice in early years settings. They are identified and explained in full in pages 11–17 of the *Curriculum guidance for the foundation stage*. The twelve principles emphasise how children learn and what practitioners need to do to support their learning (see *Chapter 2*).

## Six areas of learning

The guidance sets out six areas of learning which form the basis of the foundation stage curriculum. The areas of learning are:

1. Personal, social and emotional development (PSED)
2. Communication, language and literacy (CLL)
3. Mathematical development (MD)
4. Knowledge and understanding of the world (KUW)
5. Physical development (PD)
6. Creative development (CD).

The six areas of learning have been developed to support practitioners in their planning. We all know that young children do not categorise their learning. However, it is very important that we are aware of the content of the six areas of learning.

The contents of four of the areas of learning may seem quite obvious. Most experienced early years teachers will be quite clear about the content of personal, social and emotional development; communication, language and literacy; and mathematical and physical development. But creative development and knowledge and understanding of the world sometimes cause some confusion. Creative development does not only include art, but encompasses art, music, dance, role play and imaginative play.

The easiest way to remember the content of the final very large area of learning, knowledge and understanding of the world, is that it includes everything which is not included in the other five areas – it forms the foundation for later work in science, design and technology, history, geography, and information and communication technology (ICT).

For each of the six areas of learning, guidance is given about learning and teaching, stating clearly what effective learning involves and effective teaching requires.

## Aspects of learning

Each of the six areas of learning is divided into a number of early learning goals (*Box 1.1*). For ease, these goals are grouped together into several aspects of learning.

---

### Box 1.1 Early learning goals

---

Personal, social and emotional development (PSED)
- dispositions and attitudes
- self-confidence and self-esteem
- making relationships
- behaviour and self-control
- self-care
- sense of community.

Communication, language and literacy (CLL)
- language for communication
- language for thinking
- linking sounds and letters
- reading
- writing
- handwriting.

Mathematical development (MD)
- numbers as labels and for counting
- calculating
- shapes, space and measures.

*cont../.*

Knowledge and understanding of the world (KUW)
- exploration and investigation
- designing and making skills
- information and communication technology (ICT)
- a sense of time
- a sense of place
- cultures and beliefs.

Physical development (PD)
- movement
- a sense of space
- health and bodily awareness
- using equipment
- using tools and materials.

Creative development (CD)
- exploring media and materials
- music
- imagination
- responding to experiences and expressing and communicating ideas.

## Stepping stones

It is very important to remember that the *Curriculum guidance for the foundation stage* states that most children will achieve the early learning goals by the end of the foundation stage at the end of the reception year. By that stage, some children with August birthdays will be approaching their fifth birthday, and some children with September birthdays will be nearly six.

Children in the nursery and reception classes will, in general, be working towards the early learning goals and will be making achievements within the stepping stones. Each aspect of learning has four stepping stones towards the early learning goals. These stepping stones show the knowledge, skills, understanding and attitudes that children need to gain during the foundation stage in order to achieve the early learning goals.

The stepping stones are not age-related, although it is likely that 3-year-olds in the nursery will better described by the earlier stepping stones, shown in a yellow band. Older children in the nursery may be functioning within the next band, which is blue. Children in reception classes will often be best described by the later stepping stones in the green band, with the early learning goals in the grey band forming the final stepping stones.

## What the children can do, and the practitioner needs to do

Each spread showing the stepping stones and early learning goals also includes sections headed 'examples of what children can do' (to help practitioners assess) and 'what does the practitioner need to do?' (to help practitioners teach).

*'Use a pencil and hold it effectively to form recognisable letters, most of which are correctly formed'*, is the early learning goal for handwriting, which is one aspect of communication, language and literacy. We have to remember that this is an early learning goal, which will be achieved by the majority of children at the end of the reception year. It is now generally accepted that around 80% of children will achieve this by the end of the foundation stage, although this will depend on individual children's experiences before entering the nursery and reception classes. Younger children in

the nursery class, and those who those who are less developed in this area, will be working within the stepping stones, which are:

- engage in activities requiring hand–eye coordination use one-handed tools and equipment
  (first band, yellow)
- draw lines and circles using gross motor movement manipulate objects with increasing control
  (second band, blue)
- begin to use anticlockwise movement and retrace vertical lines, begin to form recognisable letters.
  (third band, green)

For children working within the first band, practitioners will be likely to observe achievements such as these:

- pouring water or sand from one container to another
- spreading cream cheese on to toast
- cutting clay with a blunt knife
- sieving small pebbles from dry sand.

A skilled teacher needs to be able to identify these achievements and plan experiences which will help children to consolidate their learning and extend it to the next step.

This could include:

- Providing a wide range of activities, both indoors and outdoors, which offer opportunities to pour lots of different materials on a large and small scale – large buckets and watering cans with hoses, or tiny plastic spoons and small bottles with salt and glitter.
- Providing lots of one-handed tools to manipulate playdough or other malleable materials, e.g. knives, cutters, mincer, garlic press, scissors, tweezers or tongs.

- Modelling the skills they need and offering lots of opportunities to practise those skills in non-threatening situations, e.g. using scissors in cutting and sticking activities.

## SEEING STEPS IN CHILDREN'S LEARNING

*Seeing Steps in Children's Learning* is a DVD and practitioner's guide (QCA, 2005). These have been developed to help practitioners identify where children in their own settings are achieving the stepping stones and early learning goals, identify children's learning and plan the next steps. *Seeing Steps in Children's Learning* is very closely linked to the principles for early years education and illustrates, through the learning stories of individual children, how activities can be linked to the principles to promote successful learning. Each example shows what the child is learning, how the practitioners are supporting the learning, and identifies possible next steps for consolidation and extension opportunities for individual children.

# KEY ELEMENTS OF EFFECTIVE PRACTICE

The principles for early years education are at the core of the Key Elements of Effective Practice (KEEP, DfES, 2005)*. KEEP is an evaluation tool for local authorities and illustrates the key elements of early years expertise required to implement the principles for early years education. It identifies how, through initial and ongoing training, practitioners need to develop, demonstrate and continuously improve their:

- relationships with both children and adults
- understanding of the individual and diverse ways in which children develop and learn
- knowledge and understanding in order to actively support and extend children's learning in and across all areas and aspects of learning
- practice in meeting all children's needs, learning styles and interests
- work with parents, carers and the wider community
- work with other professionals within and beyond the setting.

# TEN-YEAR STRATEGY

The government's 10-year strategy for early years and childcare, *Choice for Parents, the Best Start for Children: a Ten-year Strategy for Childcare* was published alongside the Pre-Budget Report in December 2004[†]. It sets out the government's commitment to invest in childcare, early education and work–life balance to

---

* KEEP can be downloaded from www.standards.dfes.gov.uk
  Further exemplification is available at:
  www.standards.dfes.gov.uk/primary/wholeschool/foundation_stage/

[†] Choice for Parents, the best start for children: a ten-year strategy for childcare (2004) can be accessed at www.everychildmatters.gov.uk

enable families to secure the best start in life for their children. The aim is for all parents to have access to high-quality, flexible and affordable early education and childcare for their children. The key themes are:

- Choice and flexibility
- Availability
- Quality
- Affordability.

## Choice and flexibility

Greater choice for parents to help them balance family life and work commitments through enhanced parental leave, including maternity leave entitlement and access to Sure Start Children's Centres.

## Availability

Flexible childcare for all families with children aged up to fourteen who need it, with a guarantee of care out of school hours and during the holidays between 8am and 6pm, through extended schools; 12.5 hours free early education for all three and four year old children for 33 weeks a year initially, increasing to 38 weeks a year from April 2006. From April 2007 the entitlement will be increased to 15 hours a week for the first cohort of children, with a longer term aim of 20 hours per week.

## Quality

High-quality provision which is delivered by a skilled early years education and childcare workforce with professionally-led full day care settings; a strengthened early years qualification and career structure.

## Affordability

Affordable provision appropriate to the child and family's needs with more financial support for parents, through an increase in the limits of the childcare element of Working Tax Credit.

## CHILDREN'S CENTRES

Children's Centres are at the core of the government's strategy to deliver better outcomes for children and their families. The aim is to build on the successes of the Sure Start local programmes, Early Excellence Centres and nurseries created and developed through the Neighbourhood Nursery Initiative funding to extend the benefits to all families.

Sure Start Children's Centres are an essential part of the government's 10-year childcare strategy aimed at enabling all families to have access to affordable, flexible, high-quality childcare places. The government's commitment is to deliver a Sure Start Children's Centre for every community by 2010. By March 2006, Children's Centres are expected to reach at least 650 000 pre-school children in the 20% most disadvantaged wards. The strategic responsibility for the delivery of the children's centres has been given to local authorities. Each authority has annual targets and the location and development of the centres is being planned in consultation with parents and other key partners.

Sure Start Children's Centres aim to build on good practice and are based on the concept that the provision of integrated, accessible education, care, family support and health services are key factors in determining positive outcomes for children and families.

The majority of Sure Start Children's Centres will be developed from earlier Sure Start-funded settings and other existing provision, including maintained nursery schools, primary schools and non-maintained private, community and voluntary early years settings.

Children's Centres provide flexible, multi-agency services aimed to meet the needs of young children and their families. There is a 'core offer' which includes:

- integrated early education and full day care from birth
- family support
- health services
- parental outreach services
- access to management and workforce training
- employment advice through Jobcentreplus.

Every Sure Start Children's Centre will include a qualified teacher working directly with children. Initially this is a requirement for 50% of the time, but the aim is to move as quickly as possible to a full-time teaching post. This decision has been influenced by the findings of the Effective Provision of Pre-school Education (EPPE) research (www.surestart.gov.uk/research/keyresearch/eppe). This found that the most positive educational outcomes were achieved when teachers were working directly with children and practitioners. Settings with staff with higher qualifications, especially teachers, showed higher quality and the children made more progress.

## EVERY CHILD MATTERS

*Every Child Matters: Change for Children* is a new approach to the well being of children and young people from birth to nineteen.

In 2003, the government published a green paper called *Every Child Matters* (www.everychildmatters.gov.uk), and after wide consultation published *Every Child Matters: Next Steps* (DfES, 2004) and passed the Children Act 2004. The programme places better outcomes for children at the centre of all policies and approaches involving children's services. The outcomes are:

- being healthy in both physical and mental health
- staying safe from harm and neglect
- enjoying and achieving through learning, and getting the most out of life
- making a positive contribution to society through being involved with the community and society and not engaging in offending behaviour
- achieving economic wellbeing and not being prevented from achieving full potential by economic disadvantage.

The need for change was identified in Lord Laming's report into the death of Victoria Climbié, which highlighted a need for improved integration and accountability across children's services.

## SELF-EVALUATION

Self-evaluation is a key way to develop and maintain quality in the nursery. It is an essential aspect of quality assurance. The five outcomes included in the Children Act underpin the way in which Ofsted inspections are carried out in all settings. The principles for early years education identified in the *Curriculum guidance for the foundation stage* (see *Chapter 2*) emphasise the commitment to quality and children's entitlement to high quality care and education.

*Principles into Practice* (www.principlesintopractice.org) is a self-evaluation tool. It helps teachers and all early years managers and practitioners to evaluate themselves and make judgments about the effectiveness and consistency of provision. The website is self-explanatory and has three clear audiences: practitioners working directly with children; heads and managers responsible for day-to-day organisation and monitoring; and governors, owners and others responsible for strategic development. The website raises a series of questions, based on the principles, which are aimed at promoting discussion. The framework encourages contributors at all organisational levels within the setting to respond on-line and refer to supporting documentation.

The Principles into Practice website includes a web-tool which practitioners in each early years setting can access via a password. This allows the whole staff team to monitor their progress on a regular basis. This aims to help all staff identify the strengths and areas for development within the setting, both for individuals and the whole staff team. This self-evaluation process is very flexible and designed to meet the needs of staff working in diverse settings. It is certainly not a tick-list to be worked through and then ignored. For nursery classes in schools it can help to strengthen links with the self-evaluation frameworks used in key stages 1 and 2. For teachers working in settings inspected under Section 10 of the Children Act (e.g. private or voluntary nurseries or children's centres), the process can support preparation for inspection and quality assurance accreditation.

## THE DEVELOPMENT OF A SINGLE QUALITY FRAMEWORK

The development of a single quality framework from birth to the end of the foundation stage is an essential part of the longer strategy for childcare. The 'Early Years Foundation Stage' is not intended to take the place of *Birth to Three Matters* or the *Curriculum guidance for the foundation stage*, but aims to take a 'principled approach', drawing on the principles of both and combining them so that they apply from birth to five. The framework will be linked to aspects of development and learning, the five outcomes, KEEP and relevant care standards. It aims to ensure a consistent approach to care, learning and development.

### Handy Hints

- The principles for early years education identified in the *Curriculum guidance for the foundation stage*, which became statutory in 2002, are fundamental and underpin all learning in the foundation stage.
- In the nursery, children will be working within the stepping stones, and teachers need to know where each child is in their learning and identify possible next steps for consolidation and extension.
- *Choice for Parents, the Best Start for Children: a Ten Year Strategy for Child Care* emphasises the importance of choice, flexibility, availability, quality and affordability in childcare.
- *Every Child Matters: the Next Steps* identifies five better outcomes for children which must be at the centre of all policies and approaches involving children's services:
- being healthy
- staying safe
- enjoying and achieving through learning
- making a positive contribution to society
- achieving economic wellbeing.
- Children's Centres are an essential element in the 10-year childcare strategy aimed at enabling all families to have access to affordable, flexible, high-quality childcare places.
- Self-evaluation helps practitioners, leaders and managers to develop a shared understanding of what the setting does well and what needs to be developed.
- The development of a single quality framework from birth to the end of the foundation stage is an essential part of the longer strategy for childcare.

CHAPTER 2

# WORKING WITH CHILDREN

## INTRODUCTION

The *Curriculum guidance for the foundation stage* identifies twelve principles for early years education. These are drawn from good and effective practice in early years settings and are crucial in the promotion of successful learning. They are:

1. Effective education requires both a relevant curriculum and practitioners who understand and are able to implement the curriculum requirements.

2. Effective education requires practitioners who understand that children develop rapidly during the early years – physically, intellectually, emotionally and socially. Children are entitled to provision which supports and extends knowledge, skills, understanding and confidence, and helps them to overcome any disadvantage.

3. Practitioners should ensure that all children feel included, secure and valued. They must build positive relationships with parents in order to work effectively with them and their children.

4. Early years experience should build on what children already know and can do. It should also encourage a positive attitude, a disposition to learn and aim to prevent early failure.

5. No child should be excluded or disadvantaged because of ethnicity, culture, religion, home language, family background, special educational needs, disability, gender or ability.

6. Parents or carers and practitioners should work together in an atmosphere of mutual respect within which children can have security and confidence.

7. To be effective, an early years curriculum should be carefully structured. In that structure, there should be three strands:

   - provision for the different starting points from which children develop their learning, building on what they can already do
   - relevant and appropriate content which matches the different levels of young children's needs
   - planned and purposeful activity which provides opportunities for teaching and learning, both indoors and outdoors.

8. Children should have opportunities to engage in activities planned by adults as well as those that they plan or initiate themselves. Children do not make a distinction between 'play' and 'work' and neither should practitioners. Children need time to become engrossed, to work in depth and to complete activities.

9. Practitioners must be able to observe and respond appropriately to children, informed by a knowledge of how children develop and learn. They also need a clear understanding of possible next steps in children's development and learning.

10. Well-planned, purposeful activity and appropriate intervention by practitioners will engage children in the learning process and help them to make progress in their learning.

11. For children to have rich and stimulating experiences, the learning environment should be well planned and well organised. It provides the structure for teaching within which children explore, experiment, plan and make decisions for themselves, thus enabling them to learn, develop and make good progress.

12. Above all, effective learning and development for young children requires high-quality care and education by practitioners.

These principles underpin all the work carried out in the foundation stage and are paramount to our work with children. A key theme which runs through the principles is that practitioners must be aware of what children know, can do, and are interested in. This will support children in consolidating their current learning and in planning for the next stage of learning.

# HOW CHILDREN LEARN

It is very clear that young children do not learn by being told. They are active learners, who use all their senses to begin to understand the world around them. They need first-hand experiences, both indoors and outdoors, through which they can explore, discover, observe, predict, interpret, create, investigate, hypothesise, test, practise, re-visit, discuss and make decisions.

Children need time and space to consolidate and extend their developing knowledge, understanding, skills and attitudes. This means that teachers must provide as much time as possible for uninterrupted play within the session or day. We often hear that young children can't concentrate, but when we actually take time to observe children at play, the picture can be quite different. Of course, if we disturb a child who is involved in an activity, however gently, and ask him or her to join in another adult-initiated activity, we should not be surprised if the result is a lack of concentration or a hastily- completed piece of work. Teachers need to put themselves in the position of the child. How would they feel if they were disturbed while watching a favourite television programme, or absorbed in a book, only to be asked to complete an important questionnaire or survey? We all know how annoying cold-calling is.

Young children need to be safe and secure in terms of their physical needs, but they also need to feel safe and secure emotionally. This is paramount and underpins all successful learning. They need to feel that they and their families are valued and that they belong in the nursery. It is important that they are supported as they develop into independent and autonomous individuals, and to do this they need to work within clear, shared, consistent boundaries. Of course, children will sometimes (or often) challenge these boundaries, but they feel secure in the knowledge that they are there.

Practitioners need to be clear about behavioural expectations and boundaries and must share these with families and children. A good example may be outdoor play, where one member of staff insists that children walk up the steps to the play tower, and slide down the slide. If another practitioner allows children to climb up the slide, children can become confused, particularly when they may be reminded one day 'that we always walk up the steps at nursery, it's safer', when they've been allowed to scramble up the slide minutes before.

Of course, a team discussion would elicit staff attitudes based on previous experiences: 'You can't let children clamber up slides. That happened before, and another child came down with clunky boots on and there was blood everywhere!' The important thing is that clear policies and boundaries are agreed by staff and they are implemented consistently.

Teachers need to be aware that the development of positive attitudes is as important as, or even more important than, the development of skills and the processing of knowledge. Children may learn the functions of reading, but unless they perceive themselves initially as successful learners and readers, they will rarely progress in reading or choose to read later in life. A child who chooses to pick up a book, and proceeds to act as a reader, even if the book is upside down or back to front, is far more likely to gain the necessary skills to be a successful, fluent reader.

If you feel that your initial teacher training didn't give you a clear insight into child development, take the time to read a comprehensive guide, such as: *Child Development from Birth to Eight* by Jennie Lindon (1993).

## TEACHING STRATEGIES

Visitors to nursery classes will sometimes be under the misapprehension that the children are doing exactly what they like and learning by chance. This is sometimes seen as just playing, particularly by adults who do not understand how children learn and favour a formal approach to teaching. But effective nursery learning environments are complex, well-planned and well-organised and support children's independent learning (see *Chapter 3*).

Successful nursery teachers need to develop a wide range of appropriate teaching strategies to enable children to learn (*Box 2.1*). This will involve developing sensitivity to interact and extend children's learning when it is appropriate.

Sometimes teachers become fixated on what they feel children need to learn, and fail to be sensitive to children's own learning needs and play themes.

> *For example, four children had been playing in the large block play area for over twenty minutes. They had piled all the blocks to make a tall vertical structure and had moved chairs to create a row behind the tower. They were clearly engaged in very animated role play and were making comments such as 'It's an asteroid... quick, quick, activate thrusters'. 'Red alert, red alert, we need the*

*booster rockets NOW...NOW!!'. The teacher came across the scene and approached. 'Hello, you have been busy, look at this wonderful rocket. It's so tall, is it taller than you? Silence. 'I wonder how many blocks are in the tower?' At this point two of the children drifted away from the area. The other two, after nervous glances at the teacher, decided to comply and began to count the blocks and answer the questions.*

---

### Box 2.1

---

*The Study of Pedagogical Effectiveness in Early Learning (SPEEL)* (Moyles et al, 2002) highlighted a range of teaching strategies used by practitioners:

- teaching skills and knowledge directly
- teaching through modelling behaviour
- teaching through interacting with children
- teaching through scaffolding
- teaching through communicating
- teaching through giving feedback
- teaching through questioning
- teaching through intervening
- teaching through responding to children
- motivating children and fostering their interests
- encouraging children's enquiry
- encouraging children to think about their learning.

This is an extreme but true example of the way in which teachers can disrupt rather than extend play. On this occasion, it was inappropriate to intervene with the play in any way. The most appropriate teacher role would have been to make observations of the children's learning and record the vocabulary used.

One of the key findings of the Effective Provision of Pre-school Education (EPPE) research (Effective Provision of Pre-school Education, 2003), is that:

'Good outcomes for children are linked to early years settings that provide adult-child interactions that involve open-ended questioning to extend children's thinking'.

The EPPE research set out to investigate the impact and effectiveness of pre-school settings. The statistical analysis enabled researchers to identify settings which promoted children's developmental outcomes beyond those which would be generally expected. A focus on the effective centres highlighted some key characteristics which clustered around the quality of the settings and the practice within them.

One of the most significant findings concerned the quality of adult–child interactions. The research identified sustained shared thinking as a process in which two individuals work together to solve a problem, clarify a concept or evaluate activities. Both participants contribute to the thinking, which develops and extends understanding. Sustained shared thinking involves the adult being aware of the child's interests and understanding, and working together with the child to develop an idea or skill.

To find out more, see: www.ioe.ac.uk/cdl/eppe and *Supporting Young Children's Sustained Shared Thinking* by Marion Dowling (2005).

# PLANNING AND ASSESSMENT

*Children who begin their education in a learning environment
that is vibrant, purposeful, challenging and supportive stand the
best chance of developing into confident and successful learners.
Effective learning environments are created over time as a result
of practitioners and parents working together, thinking and talking
about children's learning and planning how to promote it.*

*Good planning is the key to making children's learning effective,
exciting, varied and progressive. Good planning enables
practitioners to build up knowledge about how individual children
learn and make progress. It also provides opportunities for
practitioners to think and talk about how to sustain a successful
learning environment. This process works best when all the
practitioners working in the setting are involved.*

*Planning for Learning in the Foundation Stage*
(QCA, 2001)

Effective teaching is about meeting the needs of individual
children. It is essential to start with what children know and are
interested in, and plan the next steps for their learning.

Many inexperienced foundation stage teachers fall into the trap
of making very detailed plans based on a theme before they have
even met the children in their new class. Of course, no one can
begin a new school term without any plans at all, and sometimes
all good intentions of spending time with children and getting to
know them and their families can go awry. However, as a general
rule of thumb, planning in the foundation stage should work
on an observation-based assessment system. The underlying
principle here is that effective practitioners find out what each
individual child is like, can do, and is interested in, and then
plan possible next steps in their learning. These will include the

resources and adult support needed. This may sound daunting, but in reality experienced teachers find that there are always groups of children who have shared interests and play themes, and that there are generally groups of children who are ready for a next step of learning which is similar. This does not mean that children should be placed into groups by ability, or age. There is no place in a nursery class for 'red', 'green' or 'blue' groups for the planning of activities.

# Themes

Themes or topics have often provided a very popular basis for planning in the early years. As a new teacher in a nursery class, I was once given a folder with the class topics for the next 2 years – they included 'wheels' and 'holes'.

There is no requirement in the foundation stage to use topics as part of planning. However, many teachers and nursery teams do choose to plan around a theme. If this is the case, then the themes selected should be broad enough to include a wide variety of learning experiences and provision to support the six areas of learning. As we have already said, plans should be based on children's learning needs and interests and these should inform any theme chosen. This also means that it is more desirable in the nursery to select themes as the year develops, rather than to allocate themes on a fixed yearly cycle.

In general, themes which are broad and based on things which are familiar and relevant to children such as 'our families', 'people who help us' or 'favourite books' are likely to be far more successful than narrow, constricted themes. It is also important that themes do not become restrictive and lead to contrived and tenuous links to areas of learning. For example, one planning suggestion for a theme of water was the making of celery boats as a cooking activity. The practitioner here had clearly become obsessed with the idea of water transport and had lost sight of the basics of the theme, which in this case could easily have focused on the properties of water in cooking: dissolving ingredients in water, freezing water for ice-based recipes, boiling water with vegetables to make soup or using water as a cleaning agent.

Themes should be used to support the planning process, to give a feeling of cohesion and to help staff to be creative. Themes should not limit or restrict learning, and any thematic planning should include ongoing learning which is not theme-based.

The duration of a theme varies, but it is generally agreed that one half-term is a manageable and practical length of time. Anything shorter allows for little depth, and termly themes do not allow for children's developing interests and learning needs to be reflected.

## Role of the practitioner in planning

We have seen that the principles for early years education emphasise the importance of planning, and the *Curriculum guidance for the foundation stage* goes on to outline the role of the practitioner in planning (QCA, 2000).

Practitioners should plan:

- a learning environment, indoors and outdoors, which encourages a positive attitude to learning through rich and stimulating experiences and by ensuring each child feels included
- an environment free from stereotypical images and discriminatory practice
- resources that inspire children and encourage their own learning

- organise the learning environment to provide experiences that build on what children already know
- experiences that are relevant, imaginative, motivating, enjoyable and challenging
- to make effective use of unexpected and unforeseen opportunities for children's learning that arise from everyday events and routines
- to make good use of outdoor space so that children are enabled to learn by working on a larger, more active scale than is possible indoors
- to use their time well, so that most of it is spent directly with children
- to extend children's vocabulary and language
- to help children see the purpose of activities
- to accommodate the different ways children learn by planning for the same learning objectives in a range of ways
- to help children consolidate their learning by revisiting the same learning objectives many times
- sessions to include adult- and child-planned activities, with uninterrupted time for children to work in depth.

## Stages in curriculum planning

There are many ways of developing planning in the foundation stage, but it is generally agreed that there are three stages to curriculum planning: long-term, medium-term and short-term. What constitutes these three areas may vary between education authorities, schools or teachers, but one thing is absolutely certain – effective planning is essential and time must be made to do it.

---

## Long-term plans

Long-term plans create a framework to give structure and coherence to the curriculum and should include:

- policy statements, including information for families
- areas of provision, including the possible child-initiated learning
- the organisation of the environment, including a workshop approach to promote autonomy and independence
- rotas and routines
- a yearly overview of fixed events.

It is essential that the long-term plans underpin a learning environment which supports children's own learning, their growing independence and autonomy. This means that areas of provision should be clearly identified, planned for, resourced and maintained (see *Chapter 3*).

## Medium-term plans

*Medium-term plans bridge the gap between the broad outline of the long-term plan and the day-to-day detail of the short-term plan.*

*Planning for Learning in the Foundation Stage*
(QCA, 2001)

Medium-term plans result from team discussions and are based on children's learning needs and interests. They should be linked to long-term planning. They generally cover initial plans for learning over one half-term. As we have said, some staff teams choose to have theme-based medium- term plans, but this is not essential. Where themes are chosen, these should be as a result of children's interests and should also include plans for ongoing learning.

Medium-term plans should include:

- broad learning intentions for all six areas of learning, informed by the stepping stones and early learning goals
- ideas for experiences and provision to support the learning intentions
- other outings, visitors and events
- additional resources which will be needed
- vocabulary to be introduced or reinforced
- displays and areas of interest
- areas of provision which will be enhanced.

Medium-term plans must be flexible, working documents which develop to meet the needs of the children. There are many formats available (see *A Focus on Planning* (Lewisham Early Years Advice and Resource Network (LEARN), 2004) for photocopiable planning formats). An effective medium-term theme planner is generally A3 sized, and shows clearly the learning intentions for all six areas of learning, with possible experiences and activities identified to support the learning intentions. It is a very good idea to leave a clear surrounding area round the initial medium-term plan. This allows greater flexibility as additional plans can be written in around the plan, showing how the plans have been adapted to reflect children's interests. For example, the theme may be 'buildings', to reflect the children's initial interest in the building works that are going on within sight of the school on the local housing estate. However, if, when playing in the garden, one child finds a worm and a whole group of children become enthralled by mini-beasts, this cannot be ignored and should be reflected within the planning.

As the medium-term plans are implemented, consider highlighting the learning intentions and experiences which have actually been covered, as this serves as a record, aids evaluation and informs future planning. Medium-term plans can sometimes be very optimistic in terms of coverage, and if they really meet the needs of the children, some aspects will be developed in great depth, while others will be abandoned.

At the end of the planning period, it is essential that all team members discuss the success of the plans and evaluate, objectively, what has gone well and can be developed further and what could be changed in the future. However, it is always important to remember that while an activity might not work well with one group of children, it may work very well with another group on a different occasion.

## Short-term plans

Short-term planning should be carried out on a weekly and daily basis and should include all staff team members. Weekly plans should be flexible enough to be adapted to reflect children's developing learning needs and interests. This stage of curriculum planning must be informed by observations and assessments of children and evaluations. Short-term plans should be informed by medium-term planning and identify how staff will be deployed: *who* (staff) will be doing *what, where, when, how* and *why*.

Daily plans should include:

- learning intentions for the week across the six areas of learning, both indoors and outdoors
- a balance of adult- and child-initiated learning experiences
- clarification of how practitioners will be supporting child-initiated learning throughout the provision
- adult-focus experiences with clear learning intentions for targeted children
- resources to support all six areas of learning, indoors and outdoors.

Weekly and daily planning formats vary enormously, but should include all the information identified. The formats will often include a page for the weekly learning intentions, indoors and outdoors, and an A3 provision planner, which shows what resources will be available throughout the learning environment, and where each team member will be. It is also essential that the daily plans clearly identify learning intentions for an adult-focus activity or experience. The days are long gone when this will only focus on a creative activity, or will always occur at the activity table for the whole session and include every child. Now, the staff rota will indicate which team member is responsible for implementing the adult-focus activity. This could be a cooking activity or reading with individual children or, equally validly, planning to spend time in the role play, construction or malleable play area. Certain children may be targeted, based on their learning needs, to be included in the experience, but often other children will become involved. Conversely, the targeted children may become involved in another worthwhile activity which motivates them, and it would be inappropriate to interrupt their learning.

Adult-focus formats will usually identify:

- whether the focus is indoors or outdoors
- the staff member responsible
- how long the focus is planned for (anything between 20 minutes and the whole session)
- the area of learning focused on
- the learning intention
- any opportunities for assessment
- the targeted children
- the actual experience or activity: what the children will do
- the resources needed
- the adult input, including language to be introduced or reinforced and questions to be asked.

Effective planning can be developed through reading and learning from the experiences of others, but will really develop best through your own experiences, if you let it. Sometimes, when challenged about basic issues, teachers who have been teaching for a number of years exclaim 'but I've 20 years' teaching experience, I've always done it this way'. Don't fall into the trap of having the same experience every year for 20 years or more. Be objective about what goes well and what doesn't, learn from it and move on.

## Observation and assessment

*To help children progress, practitioners need information about what the children know, understand and can do. Through observing children at work, and by making notes when necessary about what has been achieved, practitioners can make professional judgements about their children's achievements and decide on the next steps in learning. They can also provide information for parents and carers about how children are progressing. This process, known as 'assessment for learning', is central to raising achievement. It also enhances the professionalism of practitioners by recognising their role in making judgements about their children's progress and in deciding how much record-keeping is necessary.*

*Foundation Stage Profile Handbook*
(QCA, 2003)

Effective assessment in the nursery is based on ongoing observations of children. Through accurate, objective observations we can make informed, professional judgments about children's achievements and interests and can plan the next steps in their learning.

It is essential that observations are an integral part of the daily routine in the nursery. Nursery teachers are always part of a team and may often be the team leader. It is the responsibility of the nursery team leader to monitor the quality and quantity of observations made and to ensure that time is available to discuss and evaluate the observations.

In general, there are two types of observations, short, and planned or focused:

## Short observations

These are concise, factual jottings documenting significant achievements and carried out on a daily basis. They are often observations of children involved in child-initiated activities, and can be indoors or outdoors. They are often recorded on post-it notes or on a printed format. They should include:

- date
- name of child
- name of observer
- indoor or outdoor play
- area of provision, e.g. home corner, climbing frame, creative workshop
- whether other children or adults are involved
- the area of learning covered
- what actually happened
- a verbatim record of any significant language used.

This may seem to be a lot of information, but many early years teams develop simple small formats which simply require areas to be circled and brief notes to be written down. These can be photocopied on to different coloured paper for each team member so that it is easy to identify who had written what and when (again, see LEARN (2004) for photocopiable formats).

### Planned or focused observations

These may be part of an adult-focused activity or may arise as a result of a concern about part of an individual child's development. In this case, instead of noting significant achievements as they occur, the staff team may plan to observe a child at a specific time of day, or while they are involved in a specific activity. The format will include the same information as the short observations, but may also include the planned learning intention for the specific activity or experience observed. Focused observations will generally be longer, and it is often more useful to use an A4 format so that more details can be included, such as timings where appropriate.

The most important thing about observations is that they should be useful. There is absolutely no point in having numerous observations, unread, in a pile or folder waiting to be filed. They should be used on a daily basis to inform planning, and then be kept in individual child profiles, where they inform professional judgments.

## Individual child profiles

There are many formats available for individual child profiles, but the essential aspect of all is that they should be a comprehensive record of a child's achievements across all six areas of learning. They will include observations, work samples and photographs, summaries of learning and ways forward for future learning.

An effective individual child profile will usually include:

### Background information

This is information about the child and the child's family, including languages spoken and understood, any special needs including dietary requirements, any pre-nursery experience and interests and preferred activities at home.

## Information about the settling-in process

This should usually be completed after a discussion with the parents or carers, often about 4–6 weeks after the starting date.

## Six sections – one for each of the six areas of learning

These will include any short, planned or focused observations and an aide memoire of all the stepping stones and early learning goals. These can be highlighted as children progress through the stepping stones. These sections should also include summaries based on the observations and ways forward or targets based on the summaries of learning.

## Information about any special needs

Where applicable, this will record any discussions or interventions regarding the child's special educational needs.

## Examples of children's significant achievements

This section may be stored at the back of the individual child profile in a punched plastic folder and will include photographs, drawings, mark-making and writing samples. These work samples should be clearly dated and annotated. It is important to keep photographic evidence of children's achievements in areas where drawing, mark-making and writing are not possible, and observations alone do not give the full picture, for example in role play, construction play, making music and outdoor play.

Individual child profiles provide the ongoing formative assessment which is essential for effective planning. The profiles should also be used to inform parental discussions, discussions with other professionals and to promote a smooth transition to the next stage of learning, which will often be the reception class. Teachers should use the individual child profiles to inform appropriate summaries for both parents and future teachers (see *Chapter 5*).

---

### Handy Hints

- The principles for early years education identified in the *Curriculum guidance for the foundation stage* are fundamental and underpin all learning in the foundation stage.
- Young children are active learners who need first hand experiences, both indoors and outdoors.
- Assessment for learning is central to raising achievement, and effective assessment in the nursery is based on ongoing observations of children.
- Planning in the nursery should be informed by observation-based individual child profiles.
- Long-term plans create a framework to give structure to the curriculum.
- Medium-term plans link the broad outline of the long-term plans with the detail of the short-term plans.
- Short-term plans identify who (staff) will be doing what, where, when, how and why.

CHAPTER 3

# THE LEARNING ENVIRONMENT

## INTRODUCTION

One of the most significant and easily identifiable differences a teacher can make is to the overall learning environment. Most teachers provide an environment which meets the basic needs of the children, but good teachers provide a learning environment which is stimulating, exciting and offers challenge.

It is very important to think of the indoor and outdoor provision in the nursery as one learning environment. Children should feel able to follow their own interests and play themes by moving between areas of provision, indoors and outdoors. The routine of the day should reflect this principle and allow children as much time as possible, within each session, to make their own choices and follow their own interests.

Outdoor play should be available for most of each session throughout the year. It should complement and extend indoor provision and allow children to work on a grander, larger, noisier and messier scale than indoors. It should enable them to interact with the local environment in ways which cannot happen inside. Outdoor play does allow children to develop their physical skills in ways which may be more confined indoors, by running, jumping or climbing. But outdoor play should never be confined to simply allowing children to let off steam. All six areas of learning need to be planned for so that children's learning outdoors is engaged as it is when they are indoors.

This chapter discusses how aspects of both the indoor and outdoor provision can be enhanced.

# ORGANISATION OF THE INDOOR LEARNING ENVIRONMENT

It is really important to identify clearly the areas of provision which support the six areas of learning (*Box 3.1*).*

---

## Box 3.1 Areas of provision

- home corner and role play
- creative workshop
- construction
- sand
- water
- graphics
- books
- malleable and tactile
- small world or imaginative
- music and sound-making
- mathematics
- Knowledge and understanding of the world (KUW) exploration and investigation (science and technology)
- Information and communications technology (ICT)

---

* A set of nine A3 sheets identifying some of the knowledge, skills and attitudes promoted through the areas of provision is available from Katy Elston at LEARN on 020 8695 9806.

These areas may vary, and may be given different names, but the most important thing is that the areas do exist and that both adults and children know where to go to find specific resources or to become involved in certain activities.

It is very helpful to label the areas of provision with words and photographs of children involved in the areas. These signs can be double-sided and hung from the ceilings (security systems allowing). It is also a very good idea to identify the type of independent child-initiated learning which can occur in each of the areas of provision. Staff teams should discuss the knowledge and understanding, skills and attitudes which could be developed for each of the six areas of learning through each area of provision. These lists can be supported by photographs of children learning.

It is essential that all areas of provision are:

- carefully planned for
- inviting, stimulating and challenging
- well-organised and clearly labelled
- organised to ensure resources are accessible to children and adults
- safe, clean and well-maintained.

# The workshop approach

The workshop approach is a very effective way of promoting children's autonomy and independence and encouraging them to be in control of their own learning. In a nursery which has adopted a workshop approach, practitioners ensure that a wide range of resources is available, at child height, to enable children to make independent choices to support their own learning. The resources are stored in accessible trays or boxes, clearly labelled with words and pictures so that everyone knows where to find them and, just as importantly, where to return them.

Although specific resources are stored within identified workshop areas, children use them throughout the learning environment. They should be supported, as they combine resources from different areas, to return them to the correct location when finished.

## Developing the indoor learning environment

So the environment is clean, safe and tidy, with clearly-identified, well-organised areas of provision which have labelled, accessible resources to support children's independent learning. What else needs to be done to turn an adequate learning environment into a vivid, exciting and stimulating one? Several factors play a contributory part in transforming a classroom and these include:

- displays
- the use of natural and 'real' objects
- fabrics and drapes
- presentation of resources.

## Displays

Displays help to make children and families feel part of the setting and give them a sense of belonging. Displays are not just about making the environment look nice (although that does help). They have many purposes, which include:

- sharing with families the ways in which children learn or aspects of the curriculum

- providing reference materials to support children's learning, such as number lines and alphabet posters

- celebrating children's achievements at all stages of development, thus increasing confidence and raising self-esteem

- stimulating children's curiosity and interest

- consolidating and extending children's learning

- supporting ongoing learning through the provision of positive models, giving ideas for writing forms, things which can be created with construction equipment or recycled materials

- giving children opportunities to identify and display work which is significant to them.

It is important to be creative in the use of display and to use a style which is appropriate to the purpose. For example, interactive displays stimulate children's interest and curiosity. They need to be situated at child height, on a table top or the top of a storage trolley. Where possible, displays should be sited next to a wall or display screen so that the vertical surface can also be used. Interactive displays should initially be quite simple, so that they can be developed with the children and families. An interactive display about bears may have developed because of the children's interest in the story of *The Three Bears*. The initial display could include the book, three bears, three bowls and three spoons of different sizes. As children interact with the display, they may re-tell the story or use the props to support completely different play themes. The display may stimulate them to make their own books, pictures, story props or puppets, which could be added to the display. Alternatively, practitioners could record the children's talk about the display and the story in speech bubbles (*Box 3.2*), or act as scribes for children's re-tellings of the story, which could be displayed.

---

### Box 3.2

Speech bubbles are a wonderful way of showing children that you value their talk. The speech bubbles can be computer generated, in several formats and sizes, photocopied and available for practitioners to use. As children see adults using the speech bubbles, they will often be stimulated to mark-make or write themselves, so make sure they are readily available in the graphics area.

---

### Photographs

Photographs are an integral part of most displays, and the age of digital photography has meant that they can be taken more economically and can be enlarged where necessary. It is important that process is valued more than product in the foundation stage, and photographs play an important role in this. In displays of activities such as finger painting, or model-making with recycled materials, it is possible to record the whole process and use the photographs as part of the final display.

Photographs can also celebrate children's achievements where other methods of recording are not suitable. Practitioners can record children's involvement in the role play or construction areas, offering other children ideas to support their own learning. A display of photographs of children dressing up could be entitled 'Who would you like to be today?' or photographs of children's models together with photographs of local buildings could inspire all sorts of constructions.

Laminated photographs can also be used to show a sequence of events and act as an aide memoire for some children. These could include:

- pouring a cup of water and washing up the cup
- washing hands after using the toilet
- painting a picture and transferring it to the drying rack.

## Displays for reference

When children are learning independently, they need materials to refer to when necessary. For example, the graphics area could include a display of children's mark-making and writing. A large piece of A1 coloured card can be labelled 'What will you write today?' and have ideas spaced out over it, such as 'an envelope', 'a label', 'a postcard', 'a shopping list' and 'a book'. The card can then be laminated, and once created will form the background for a permanent, changeable display. Examples of children's achievements when making books, writing postcards or shopping lists can be fixed to the display using Blu Tack and changed when appropriate.

Children also need access to relevant, meaningful number lines and alphabets. A simple number line can be made using photographs of the children from the nursery (see *Chapter 4*). The most meaningful alphabet charts include upper and lower case letters with familiar photographs as picture clues. An alphabet line can made by printing out one upper case and lower case letter on each of 26 A4 cards and adding photographs of children whose names begin with the letter, together with familiar objects which start with the same letter. This line can be created with the children to ensure they have ownership of the finished resource.

## Children's own displays

Teachers often involve children in creating displays and encourage them to develop interactive displays. However, it is a very good idea to have an area where children can display their own work independently. This could be a cork notice board (the sort with crossed-over tapes) on the back of a door, a pin board or a section of wall where achievements can be fixed with Blu Tack. The area can be clearly labelled 'all our own work' and include a short explanation for adults: 'Here are some pieces of our own work. We are proud of them'. This display area gives children a feeling of instant success and can give teachers a different perspective of children's views on their own learning.

## Using natural and real objects

Children are surrounded at home by plastic toys. You only have to look in supermarkets, department stores or catalogues to be convinced of this. Of course, toys made of wood and other natural resources are available but they are often seen as more expensive, less durable and more difficult to keep clean. Moreover, many children are less likely, now than ever before, to have opportunities to play outside in parks or the countryside and to interact with natural resources such as mud, puddles, ponds, rocks, plants, pebbles, shells, sand, twigs, branches, tree stumps, boulders or mini-beasts. For many children opportunities to build tree houses, swing from branches on ropes, pond dip, build dens in secret places, collect ladybirds in jam jars or make petal perfume, have never existed. This is because 'outdoors' is often perceived by parents as unsafe for a number of reasons, often over-stated by the media.

So it is very important that children have opportunities to interact with natural materials at nursery. Of course sand is available daily, in different forms including dry, damp and wet. But other natural resources can be used to support imaginative play. Rocks, logs, fir cones, shells, pebbles, leaves and plants can be added to sand trays or other imaginative play scenarios to create a more exciting play situation and give children opportunities to explore the properties of natural resources. Children should also have access to imaginative play scenarios which include potting compost, cocoa shells, wood chips or shavings (see *Chapter 4*).

## Plants and animals

Children need opportunities to find out more about living things as these form part of their knowledge and understanding of the world. Growing plants, both indoors and outdoors, can be an excellent way of developing their understanding of the needs of

living things. Pot plants such as spider plants, tradescantia and lemon balm are particularly good in nurseries as they are very resilient and if pieces are broken accidentally, they can be used as cuttings since they grow new roots when placed in water. The plants also make really worthwhile additions to imaginative play scenarios.

Plants are aesthetically pleasing to the eye and will enhance the environment, but it is also important that children take responsibility for their care and maintenance. Teachers need to provide experiences which help children understand that plants need warmth, water and light to grow. Plants need regular watering and it may be appropriate to establish a watering rota so that children provide enough, but not too much, water.

Bulbs and seeds are a wonderful way to support children's understanding of growth. Cress, runner beans and amaryllis bulbs grow so quickly that even the most impatient child will be satisfied. A vegetable garden, or plants in containers outdoors, can provide children with opportunities to explore digging and growing on a much larger scale.

Nursery or school policies about animals will vary enormously, and teachers should of course be informed by these. If it is decided that it is appropriate to keep a pet, practitioners must carefully consider the consequences. 'A dog is for life, not just for Christmas' and the same applies to pets in nurseries. Someone must take responsibility for the pet, and ensure that its quality of life is always the best possible, including during weekends and holidays. Animals should not be left alone other than overnight. However, there are very few experiences guaranteed to inspire awe and wonder more readily than the birth of a baby and the development to adulthood. Of the small mammals, guinea pigs are generally the most successful, as they are awake in the daytime, tend to be less smelly and give birth to young with fur and open eyes.

Many nurseries choose to keep fish as an alternative to other pets. It is important to consider the learning potential of keeping any living things. It is not enough to provide a suitable tank, with a pump and plants, feed and clean the fish regularly and simply leave them in the corner. Children need to be involved in the care of the fish, and this offers opportunities to develop a feeding rota which children can complete with adults. The tank should be surrounded by pictures children have drawn, speech bubbles recording comments they have made, and information texts about fish. Children should be encouraged to observe the fish and to notice changes in their behaviour.

Ducks and chickens can be incubated in nurseries and Aylesbury ducks (the big white ones) mature to adulthood within 6 weeks of hatching. It is often possible to purchase partially incubated eggs from farms. This means a greater chance of successful incubation and a shorter wait until hatching.

As with all living things in the nursery, be quite clear about the level of commitment needed and ensure you have the right resources and information before you start. It is important to find an appropriate home for the ducks or chickens before you acquire them. One thing is certain; you are highly unlikely to want to return your hand-reared adults to a commercial farm where they are likely to become dinner. The RSPCA offers advice about the care of animals (www.rspca.org.uk).

Mini-beasts from the outdoor area can easily be temporarily accommodated indoors, as long as they have a suitable habitat and food. However, they should always be returned to their original habitat. Life-cycles can be studied through the observation of eggs, caterpillars, pupae or chrysalises, butterflies, moths or frogspawn, tadpoles, froglets and frogs. Insectlore supply lots of resources to support the study of life-cycles (www.insectlore. co.uk; see useful websites in the *Bibliography*).

## Fabrics and drapes

Fabrics and drapes can be used in a variety of ways to make the environment a softer, more welcoming place. Of course, fabric lengths can be used as the focal point of a display, or to cover storage units or table tops as a display background. In this case they may be thematically based – with numbers, animals or vegetable designs. Bright, colourful plain and patterned fabrics also play a role in developing a stimulating environment. But fabrics also have the added advantage of giving children opportunities to explore different textures. Hessian, fun fur, velvet, brocade, denim, embroidered, silky or shiny fabrics all have a place in the nursery. Try using different fabrics as table covers, fixing them with table clips. They will make the room look more inviting and also cut down the noise level, particularly if used with construction equipment (carpet and lino off-cuts can be used in the same way).

You can create a collection of fabric lengths without spending too much money. Try asking family members to search at home for unwanted curtain or dressmaking remains, or scour the local markets for remnants. With any luck, you may discover someone who has a hidden talent for making costumes for stage productions and has the most unlikely fabrics hidden away.

Alternatively, collect unwanted clean white cotton sheets and plan cooperative creative activities which involve the methods of tie-dying, printing, drawing with fabric crayons or cold water batik (*Box 3.3*).

## Presentation

When they are encouraged to be, young children are autonomous, independent learners who will select resources to support their own learning. However, it is also the role of the adult to present resources to children in a way which will inspire and motivate them.

---

**Box 3.3**

---

To make cold water paste batik with the children:
- mix up a very thick batter using flour and water
- the children dip their hands into the paste and make hand prints on the fabric
- the flour paste dries
- the fabric is dyed using cold water dyes and washed in hot water to remove the flour paste.

A set of model wild animals can be left in a box on a table, or tipped out onto a carpet, or it can be presented in a much more exciting, vibrant way. A piece of fake grass can form the base of a jungle which includes tree stumps, logs, boulders, plants and other natural objects, where the wild animals can be hidden (see *Chapter 4*).

Again, you can easily collect resources to supplement imaginative play materials (*Box 3.4*) or create a generally more interesting learning environment (*Box 3.5*). But it does require careful organisation. First, be quite clear about what you want to collect, and then make a large poster for display, with a list of resources and where possible, real examples. Fix what you want to collect, for example an empty film canister, washing liquid ball, washing tablet net bag or snack pot container, to the poster. Then ask colleagues, the children and family members to collect the resources needed. It is important to store the resources in clearly marked boxes which can be easily accessed as needed.

---

### Box 3.4 Free materials to support exploratory and imaginative

Make collections of:

- coins
- stamps
- fir cones
- shells
- washing tablet nets
- washing liquid balls
- mini snack containers
- film canisters
- biscuit and sweet tins
- assorted cardboard cartons
- chocolate boxes and liners
- wicker baskets
- buttons
- cotton reels
- shiny gift bags and boxes
- bright wrapping paper
- plant cuttings
- plastic bottles
- ribbons
- clothes pegs
- cake cases
- birthday candles
- kitchen utensils
- conkers
- leaves
- locks and keys
- roll-on bottles
- squeezy bottles
- rope, string and cord
- wool
- brushes
- marbles

---

> ### Box 3.5 Free materials to create a stimulating learning environment
>
> Make collections of:
>
> - wrapping paper
> - wallpaper
> - wallpaper borders
> - fabric
> - magazine pictures
> - photographs
> - mirrors
> - plants
> - plant cuttings
> - seeds and bulbs
> - wicker baskets
> - wooden bowls.

## DEVELOPING THE OUTDOOR AREA

Many of the principles which underpin the development of an exciting and challenging learning environment apply both indoors and outdoors. It is possible to present almost every indoor learning experience in a similar way outdoors. This may well have advantages for some children who prefer to spend time outdoors. They may choose to sit at a table and draw a picture, play with a small construction toy or read a book outdoors, when they would rarely choose to do so inside. Teachers need to capitalise on the very nature of the outdoor area and extend experiences children may have indoors with experiences on a larger, messier, noisier and generally grander scale.

The workshop approach should be adopted outdoors in the same way as indoors and all resources should be clearly labelled with words and pictures. Wherever possible, the storage should be weather-resistant and durable, as it will often be outdoors during inclement weather.

One very good way of considering the development of the outdoor area is to consider experiences which can support children's development across the six areas of learning. The aim should be to complement and extend, rather than repeat, indoor provision. Teachers should ensure that appropriate resources are available to support child-initiated learning and should plan appropriate adult-initiated learning experiences outdoors.

## Personal, social and emotional development

The following will encourage personal, social and emotional development:

- cooperating and sharing wheeled toys and large equipment
- working together when moving large blocks or buckets of water or sand
- creating and implementing shared rules for games
- playing ring games
- beginning to understand the needs of living things
- exploring and taking risks within a safe and secure outdoor environment
- selecting and using resources and activities independently
- showing care and concern for others and the environment
- putting on and taking off outdoor clothing independently
- taking turns using equipment.

## Communication, language and literacy

The outdoor setting can be used to enhance communication, language and literacy by:

- re-telling stories, for example by using an upturned see-saw or large wooden blocks as a bridge for the Billy Goats Gruff
- playing games such as 'heads, shoulders, knees and toes'
- using huge laminated alphabet charts, including clues for natural objects or things which can be seen outdoors
- using water, buckets and decorators' brushes to paint on walls or the floor
- using playground chalks to make marks on designated areas of the wall or ground
- using information texts to support outdoor learning about trees, plants, mini-beasts or travel
- mark-making on a huge scale using large chalk boards (*Box 3.6*) or strips of lining-paper fixed to a wall or fence, or on the ground
- running with streamers and making patterns in the air to promote early writing
- calling out names and hearing syllables in words
- repeating and creating rhythms using wooden spoons and plastic buckets and bowls as drums
- using language to recreate roles and experiences while involved in outdoor role play scenarios.

---

### Box 3.6 Create a large scale chalk board:

1. Buy external plywood, which large DIY stores will often cut to size.
2. Seal both sides and all the edges with yacht varnish.
3. Fix to the wall.
4. Paint the front with chalkboard paint.
5. Fix two cup hooks to hold a chalk tray and cloths.
6. Add two bull dog clips which can hold large pieces of paper.

# Mathematical development

Mathematical development can be promoted by:

- using number lines, with real natural objects, or threaded with ribbon or shredded green plastic bags into open mesh fences
- parking numbered wheeled toys in parking bays labelled with numerals
- returning resources to numbered storage containers
- acting out number rhymes on a large and noisy scale, for example five little frogs jumping off real logs
- making collections of natural objects, sorting, sequencing or counting them
- recognising patterns and shapes in the environment
- understanding size by being inside large boxes or hidey-holes
- experiencing being under, over, through or next to climbing equipment and understanding or using positional language
- playing games which involve moving between chalked colours, shapes or numerals
- manipulating much larger three-dimensional shapes such as crates and boxes
- exploring measures and experiencing heavy weights such as sand, gravel or water
- using painted or chalked number lines or tracks
- scoring games with balls, beanbags, quoits, skittles or hoops (Make skittles by filling bottles with water or sand. Create a target using aluminium foil – children can hear as well as see when they score.)
- playing 'What's the time Mr Wolf?'.

## Knowledge and understanding of the world

Children's knowledge and understanding of the world can be increased by:

- collecting and investigating natural objects such as leaves and pebbles
- making rubbings of different surfaces
- using maps of the local environment in role play
- observing the life cycle of vegetables and other plants
- exploring sand, water and other tactile substances on a large scale
- noticing and commenting on changes in the environment, such as trees
- observing and commenting on vehicles on adjoining roads, such as lorries and cars or aeroplanes in the sky
- construction using A-frames, wooden pallets, tyres, long strips of fabric and large cardboard boxes
- noticing signs and symbols in the environment

- using magnifying glasses to observe mini-beasts in their natural environment
- investigating puddles and shadows.

## Physical development

Physical development can be stimulated by:

- sweeping up puddles
- digging and using gardening equipment
- negotiating space when playing chasing and racing games
- exploring different ways of moving
- jumping off tree stumps
- travelling around, under, over and through climbing equipment
- using small equipment such as bats, balls, quoits, beanbags and hoops, with or without targets
- children noticing the changes in their bodies when involved in active play
- using large-wheeled toys.

## Creative development

Creative development will be encouraged by:

- using saucepans, metal bins, plastic bowls and buckets and wooden spoons to create rhythms
- painting with water in decorators' buckets
- drawing with chalks on designated areas of the wall and the ground
- painting with large brushes on lining paper
- making footprints with bare feet or wellington boots, paint and wallpaper strips

- becoming involved in outdoor role play scenarios
- dancing and moving on a large scale to music
- recognising shapes, colours and textures in the environment and responding to them
- using crayons to make rubbings
- making dens to support role play.

## Free materials to support large scale outdoor play

### Make collections of

- guttering and plastic pipes
- tyres
- plastic crates
- tree trunk sections
- cardboard packing cases
- blankets, rugs, sheets and duvet covers
- lengths of fabric
- plastic buckets and bowls
- shiny things
- saucepans and other cooking utensils
- wooden pallets
- large wooden boxes
- leftover wallpaper
- rope
- steering wheels

## Handy Hints

- Areas of provision to support the six areas of learning should be clearly identified and resourced.
- The workshop approach promotes children's autonomy and independence and encourages them to be in control of their own learning.
- An exciting, challenging and stimulating learning environment can be developed through the creative use of photographs, displays, natural and real objects, fabrics and drapes.
- Indoor and outdoor provision in nursery should be thought of as one learning environment. Children should feel able to follow their own interests and play themes by moving between areas of provision.
- Outdoor play should be available for most of each session and throughout the year. It should complement and extend indoor provision and allow children to work on a grander, larger, noisier and messier scale than indoors.

CHAPTER 4

# LEARNING EXPERIENCES AND ACTIVITIES

## INTRODUCTION

*There should be opportunities to engage in activities planned by adults and also those that they (children) plan or initiate themselves*

*Curriculum guidance for the foundation stage*
(QCA, 2003)

The foundation stage is, in many ways, unlike any other key stage in children's education. Teachers are very clear about the knowledge and understanding, skills and attitudes which children need to develop in order to be successful, competent learners and they know that children learn by being active learners.

However, it has sometimes been seen that early years practitioners should set the scene, provide the resources and then stand back and observe what happens. But this is clearly not the case. Teachers have a huge and varied role in supporting children's learning, which includes ensuring a careful balance between adult-initiated and child-initiated experiences. Research has shown that practitioners in the most successful settings do plan for adult-initiated activities, but also encourage, support and extend child-initiated experiences.

*In the 'excellent' settings, the balance of who initiated the activities (staff members or child) was nearly equal, revealing that the pedagogy of the excellent settings encourages children to initiate activities as often as the staff. Also, staff regularly*

*extended child-initiated activities, but did not dominate them...
Freely chosen play activities often provided the best opportunities
for adults to extend children's thinking. Adults need, therefore,
to create opportunities to extend child-initiated play as well
as teacher-initiated group work, as both have been found to be
important for promoting learning.*

(Effective Provision of Pre-school Education, 2003)

Therefore it is essential that the nursery team plans together to ensure there is a good balance between appropriate, exciting activities initiated by adults and a carefully planned learning environment, with clearly identified areas of provision, which supports child-initiated experiences.

Of course, if the adult-initiated activities are well-matched to children's interests, it is likely that they will want to repeat or extend them. It is therefore essential that practitioners carefully plan the environment so that children can use the available resources to revisit experiences independently.

This chapter aims to offer ideas for developing and enhancing some areas of provision and ideas for adult-initiated activities to support the six areas of learning.

## CORE AND ENHANCED PROVISION

We initially identified the main areas of provision in *Chapter 3*. Of course, all of these areas will be well resourced and maintained, with clearly labelled, accessible resources. Some of the areas, such as the book area, home corner and creative workshop can be seen as core provision. That is to say, the same high-quality resources will be available every day in the areas over a long period of time. This ensures continuity and allows children to revisit experiences, extend and develop play themes and consolidate their learning. For example, the graphics workshop should always include, as an absolute minimum, these resources:

- envelopes and business stationery
- paper in assorted shapes, sizes, colours, both lined and plain
- assorted mark-making tools, for example pencils, fibre-tipped markers, crayons
- sellotape, glue sticks, masking tape, hole punch, staple-less stapler
- clipboards with pencils attached
- name cards
- alphabet chart with upper and lower case letters and picture clues
- examples of completed writing formats such as greetings cards, books, letters, invitations and lists.

In addition to the core resources teachers will, at times, choose to enhance the core provision. This will often be as a result of observations of children which indicate their learning interests and needs. For example, if children have shown an interest in postcards following holidays, the following could be added to the graphics area:

- used postage stamps
- a post box, either plastic or made from a cardboard box covered in red paper
- assorted new picture postcards
- writing formats of a simple postcard
- used postcards.

Alternatively, practitioners may identify that an area of core provision is being under-used and plan to enhance the provision to support a current theme. For example, the home corner may include a wide variety of resources, but to support a theme on water the following could be added:

- vase and silk flowers
- window box
- watering can
- fish tank and accessories
- plastic potted plants
- new washing up bowl, bucket and mop
- washing line and pegs.

## Developing the role play area

Children function at their highest level when they are engaged in play themes and activities of their own choice. This is why well-planned role play is such an effective way of supporting children's development across all six areas of learning.

It is important to allow as much space as possible for home corner and role play provision. It is simply not enough to provide a few battered dolls, a cradle, a cooker and some mismatched cups and saucers. Children need access to a basic, well-resourced home corner, indoors and everyday (*Box 4.1*). Where possible, a similar house should be provided outdoors (*Box 4.2*). Additionally, teachers should plan to either enhance the home corner provision on a regular basis, or to provide an additional role play area. The areas complement each other. A shop, clinic, animal hospital or take-away will extend children's play as they take the pet dog or baby to and from the clinic or veterinary surgery, or unpack the shopping or take-away food. Of course if space is limited, the home corner may have to be reduced in size to accommodate the additional role play, but it is important that it remains. Some role play areas are more logically sited outdoors and often give children opportunities to develop their role play in much larger, noisier, physical ways than indoors.

## Box 4.1 Ideas for indoor role play areas

- baby clinic
- hospital
- doctors surgery
- office
- veterinary surgery
- theatre
- post office

- museum
- estate agent
- optician
- party
- library
- launderette
- hairdresser

**eating places:**
- Indian
- Chinese
- Italian
- vegetarian

- pizza
- café
- fast food
- fish and chips

**shops:**
- clothes
- shoe
- hat
- toy
- supermarket
- baker

- greengrocer
- pet
- wedding
- fancy dress
- florist

---

## Box 4.2 Ideas for outdoor role play areas

- airport
- fire station
- market stall
- building site
- garage
- car wash
- garden party
- garden centre
- band stand
- desert island
- cave
- picnic
- train station
- spaceship
- ship
- camping
- castle
- bus station
- farm
- safari park
- beach

We have already discussed enhancing home corner role play, and time can be saved in the long run if resources are collected and stored before they are needed (*Box 4.3*). Wherever possible, it is better to use real objects rather than plastic substitutes from education catalogues, as long as they are safe and properly maintained (always cut the leads and plugs off electrical equipment such as hairdryers, radios or lamps).

---

> ## Box 4.3 Free materials to support home corner role play
>
> Make collections of:
>
> - television guides
> - A-Z maps
> - telephones and mobiles
> - a message board
> - telephone pads
> - address books
> - calendars
> - recipe books
> - cameras
> - telephone directories
> - take-away menus
> - junk mail cards and forms
> - unwanted kitchen utensils
> - hats, scarves and bags
> - vases, photo frames and pictures
> - silk and plastic flowers
> - cookery books.

When developing a particular role play area, it is always a good idea to visit the relevant place and look out for elements which can be re-created, paying attention to resources which are specific to the setting. Wherever possible, discuss what you are doing with someone who works on site. It is often surprising what resources they are able to gather and donate. Large scale London Underground maps, pocket maps, timetables, leaflets, used tickets, signs and even railway hats from a station would be useful. Numerous resources from post offices, shops, clinics and veterinary surgeons often result from a friendly chat. Never underestimate the impact of working closely with families (see *Chapter 5*). Also ensure that families know when you are planning to develop a role play area so that they can contribute if they have contacts. Where storage space is available, it is very worthwhile keeping key resources in clearly marked boxes, with lists of other replaceable resources which have been collected in the past, for future use.

# DEVELOPING TACTILE AND MALLEABLE PROVISION

Children need plenty of opportunities to explore and discover the properties of materials. This can include finding out what happens when things are used in water or sand, but should also include time to experiment with malleable and tactile materials. These can be offered to children in a wide variety of ways, for example on a small scale in a cat litter tray or on a large scale in a black tray or deep sand tray. The way in which resources are offered to children will influence the way in which they use them. Large objects in large containers will help support the development of large motor skills and the use of tiny objects will help to develop fine motor skills, which are needed later for writing.

Many nurseries have policies about the use of food products, and practitioners sometimes have very strong views about this. If there is no policy, then create one after consultation with families and colleagues. In the majority of nurseries it is usually acceptable to use basic ingredients in a sensible way, while most practitioners would draw the line at baked bean, mashed potato or jelly play.

## Malleable and tactile experiences

- sand mousse (*Box 4.4*)
- damp and wet red, grey and self-hardening clay
- cornflour and water
- play dough (*Box 4.5*)
- dry, damp and wet sand
- potting compost

- bark chips and wood shavings
- cocoa shells
- gravel and pebbles
- cooked or uncooked pasta shapes and spaghetti
- salt
- lentils, peas, rice or butter beans
- Plasticene
- pure soap flakes and water (whisked to a gel)
- hypoallergenic shaving foam (with or without paint)
- non-fungicidal paste and paint.

---

**Box 4.4**

---

Make sand mousse for children to explore by adding hypoallergenic bubble bath and a small amount of water to dry sand. The sand can be dried out later and re-used, but it will have a more powdery texture.

---

## The wonder of play dough

Ready-made play dough can be readily purchased at a cost, but it is much more fun to provide a variety of home-made play dough (*Box 4.5*). On occasions, this can be made with the children, as part of an adult-initiated activity which supports children's knowledge and understanding of the world. But at other times it is appropriate to give children ready-to-use dough to explore. Play dough shouldn't be limited to the usual pastel colours; let your imagination run wild and add colours, textures and aromas.

## Box 4.5 Basic play dough recipe

- 2 cups plain flour
- 2 cups water
- 1 cup salt
- 2 teaspoons cream of tartar
- 2 tablespoons cooking oil
- A few drops of food colouring and/or essence.

Put all the ingredients into a large saucepan and mix them together.

Cook over a moderate heat, stirring continuously. Don't worry if the mixture becomes lumpy.

When the mixture begins to form a ball, remove from the saucepan and allow to cool.

Knead the dough until smooth.

The dough will keep for several weeks in an airtight container in the refrigerator.

### Play dough is great dough

Try adding:

- bright fluorescent paint
- black paint and glitter
- sequins
- rice or tiny pasta shapes
- granary flour
- green colouring and peppermint essence
- orange colouring and orange essence

- yellow colouring and lemon essence
- red colouring and strawberry essence
- brown colouring and liquid concentrated coffee.

## Provide resources to support play themes

- rolling pins, cutters, cutting boards and place mats
- cake trays, candles and paper cake cases
- icing tools, garlic press, potato masher and tongs
- cooker, hob, cooking utensils
- tea set and picnic basket
- plates, bowls, chop-sticks, knives, forks and spoons
- plastic hammers and wooden mallets
- clay tools
- scissors and blunt knives
- chocolate boxes and tiny cutters
- plastic eggs, twigs and feathers
- lolly sticks and straws.

Malleable and tactile activities can be presented in a variety of ways, in shallow or deep, large or small trays designed for the purpose. However, there are a number of really versatile trays available which were originally designed for gardening, home or building purposes. These can be found in most large DIY and garden centres, and some are now available from educational suppliers.

**Potting tray:** originally designed for potting seedlings in green house, this is a smaller square tray with a higher back than front, deeper than the other trays, ideal for creating small-scale imaginative play scenarios.

**Black tray/Tuff spot:** originally designed as a surface to mix concrete, the largest, most durable and versatile tray, about a metre square.

**Grow bag tray:** exactly the size of a standard grow bag, equally useful on a single table or the floor.

**Cat litter tray:** ideal for small-scale play activities and available in lots of bright colours.

## Making the most of a black tray

Black trays are very flexible and durable so don't be afraid to put a wooden block or a large ball of old Plasticene under one corner to give children opportunities to experience different levels. This means that one part can have water in and another part can be filled with dry compost or sand. Some of the resources may be hard to track down, but some suggestions are given in the resources section of the bibliography. The sides of the black tray also make it a practical resource for keeping things together such as:

- marbles
- threading-beads or cotton reels
- dry pasta, scoops and bowls
- sorting buttons
- programmable or remote controlled toys.

Try these ideas and use your imagination and the children's to add more resources.

### Create small world or imaginative play scenarios

- ice cubes and or snow, artic creatures, blue gauze, shells, branches and boulders (Make friends with staff in a take-away outlet which has an ice-maker. Arrange to collect a carrier bag or two of ice.)
- sand, water, boats and people to make a seaside

- sand, water, gravel, boulders, potted plants, branches, pebbles, shells and wild animals
- ice cubes and treasure or small creatures frozen in ice (place the items in assorted bowls, fill with water, and freeze overnight)
- cut grass, hay, wooden fences, farm house, farm animals
- potting compost, watering cans, plastic and silk flowers, trowels, flower pots
- potting compost, watering cans, leaves and plastic mini-beasts
- water, gravel, glass pebbles, shells, log and five plastic frogs
- water, metallic gravel, glass pebbles, plastic or silk water lilies, numerals one to five, one plastic duck and five ducklings
- water, gravel, pebbles, rocks, potted plants, shells, sea creatures
- potting compost, boulders, fir cones, branches, potted plants and dinosaurs
- sand, small plastic trees, metal foil container of water, camels and people
- sand, sieves, treasure chests, gold coins, jewellery and beads
- grow grass seed in the tray and create a farm or jungle with real grass
- wood shavings, hay, toy rabbits or guinea pigs, brush, food bowl and pet water bottle
- wooden or plastic bricks, sand, construction workers and diggers and dumpers
- soap flakes, whisked in warm water, some coloured green and some brown, logs, stones, potted plants, fir cones, dinosaurs
- sand, potted plants, dolls, small cups, saucers and plates, a square of checked fabric

- water, metallic gravel, glass pebbles, fishing nets and plastic fish
- fake grass in one half of tray, sand in a quarter and water in the final part, with plastic people and plastic playground set
- display netting rocks, plastic snakes and potted plants
- silver foil blanket, moonglow gravel, moonstone black pebbles, boulders, space station, and space travellers
- resources to re-tell children's favourite stories, which will often involve a journey, such as: *The Train Ride, Handa's Surprise, Rosie's Walk or We're Going on a Bear Hunt.*

## Give children opportunities to explore materials

Children will enjoy experimenting with:

- snow, ice and diluted colouring in small bottles with droppers
- water and sandwich bags full of diluted colouring (to burst)
- water and crepe paper strips (see what happens)
- clay, water, squeezy bottles, wooden mallets
- wood shavings, twigs, tree trunk sections, branches
- ready-mixed paint and plastic cars
- ready-mixed paint and mark-making tools
- powder paint, droppers, small bottles of water to finger paint
- hypoallergenic shaving foam and powder paint to finger paint
- natural soap flakes, limited warm water and whisks
- dry pasta and bowls
- cooked pasta and saucepans.

# ADULT-INITIATED EXPERIENCES

The following adult-initiated experiences, which cover the six areas of learning, have been included either because each activity is a firm favourite, which can be revisited again and again and developed over time, or because it is more unusual and may not have been considered.

These experiences are ones which would be called 'adult focus' activities (see *Chapter 2*). It is important to remember that these experiences should be introduced in response to children's interests and learning needs and should generally be aimed at targeted children. They may best be implemented with individual children, pairs or a small group. If an activity is likely to include a larger group, it is important to plan for two or more adults to be involved, to support the younger or less-developed children where necessary.

Whenever adult focus activities are planned, it is important to identify one clear learning intention linked to the stepping stones for one of the six areas of learning. We all know that making play dough with children could cover a number of learning intentions across the areas, but it is important to be clear what the focus is on this particular occasion.

## Making bird cake

**Learning intention:** Personal, social and emotional – to work as part of a group, taking turns.

**Resources:** Wild bird seed, raisins and peanuts; suet which is at room temperature; yoghurt pots; string; mixing bowl and wooden spoon; scissors.

**What to do:** Talk to the children about the birds in the outdoor area and the things they like to eat. Explain that in the winter birds sometimes need some help finding enough food and water. Give the children lots of opportunities to explore and discuss the bird seed and other resources. Explain that you are going to make bird cake.

Make a small hole in the bottom of each yoghurt pot, just large enough to thread the string through and tie a knot inside. Make sure there is enough string to hang the pots on the bird table or tree. Add the ingredients to the suet in the mixing bowl and stir with a spoon. Fill the yoghurt pots with the mixture and chill in the refrigerator for several hours. Hang the bird cakes in safe places away from cats.

## Extensions

- Provide clip boards, pens and laminated bird identification cards to encourage children to record the birds they have seen in the outdoors area or eating the bird cake.
- Encourage the children to take digital photographs of the birds they observe, and use speech bubbles to record their comments.

## Teddy Bear Hunt

**Learning intention:** Communication, language and literacy – to sustain attentive listening, responding to what the children have heard by relevant actions.

**Resources:** Several teddy bears.

**What to do:** Hide one teddy bear somewhere in the outside area. Explain to the children that they are going on a teddy bear hunt. Explain the rules: they have to crawl or walk very slowly and carefully, so that they don't scare the teddy bear. The adult gives the children clues, very quietly when they are a long way from the teddy bear and more loudly as they get closer. For example (whisper)

'Ibrahim, you are very cold'; 'Sam, you are freezing'; (louder) 'Hayriye, you are getting warmer, and warmer still'. Continue until the teddy bear is found. Everyone covers their eyes while another teddy bear is hidden. When the children are confident with giving instructions, encourage them to take the lead.

### Extensions

- Play the game using movements from *We're Going On A Bear Hunt*.
- Give robot instructions to the children from a specific starting point: two steps forward...turn towards the tree... three steps forward...

## Creating a number line

**Learning intention:** Mathematical development − to recognise numerals 1-5.

**Resources:** A selection of cut-out photographs of children in the group; five A4 pieces of coloured card; number reference books.

**What to do:** Print one numeral from 1 to 5 on each of the A4 card sheets. Look at the photographs and books and discuss them with the children. Look at each numeral, and identify it together, counting out the correct number of photographs to match. Stick one picture on the card labelled with numeral '1', two for the '2' card, and so on until the number line is complete. Laminate the cards and place them at child height in the maths area.

### Extensions

- Support children making their own zigzag number books with drawings.

- Make another laminated number line for the outdoor area, or make a line 1-10.
- Laminate five A4 cards with the numerals 1-5 and support children as they collect the correct number of objects (small plastic mini-beasts or counters) and fix them to the card with blu-tack.

# Five currant buns

**Learning intention:** Mathematical development – to say and use number names in order in familiar contexts

**You will need:** Five salt dough buns; five plastic coins; a chef's hat;

**What to do:** Introduce the rhyme to the children. Repeat this over several days and encourage them to join in with the words. Once the children have begun to be familiar with the rhyme, encourage them to act it out. Choose five children, each to hold a currant bun, five children, each to hold a coin, and one child to be the baker and wear the chef's hat. The five children with currant buns and the baker stand at the front of the group as the rhyme is sung. Then the adult chooses one child with a coin to buy a currant bun and take it away, paying the baker with the coin. The rhyme continues until all of the buns have been bought. The rhyme has many versions, but this is one of the most frequently used:

5 currant buns in a baker's shop;
Round and fat with sugar on the top.
Along came *Laurie** with a penny one day,
Bought a currant bun and took it right away.
(*insert appropriate child's name)
4 currant buns...........

## Extensions

- Encourage the children to re-tell the rhyme independently, either using the cooked salt dough buns or magnetic props to support them.
- Introduce other counting rhymes in a similar way, using appropriate props.

# A cottage for the *Three Little Pigs*

**Learning intention:** Knowledge and understanding of the world – to design and make things for a purpose.

**Resources:** Three plastic pigs, or pig finger puppets; Lego bases and bricks; clipboards and pencils.

**What to do:** Ensure the children are familiar with the story of the Three Little Pigs. Discuss what sort of house the pigs would need if they all lived together after the wolf had gone. How many bedrooms? What other rooms are needed? Encourage the children to select bases and bricks to make a cottage for the pigs, considering their needs. When the cottages are complete, discuss how the children can record their work by drawing plans of the building. Some children may find it easier to include a verbal list of instructions and an adult should act as scribe where necessary.

## Extensions

- Carry out a similar activity using soft toys and large wooden blocks or empty boxes. Take photographs rather than making written plans.
- Provide a simple writing format for children to record their constructions independently, and make these available on

clipboards in the construction area. Include a space for a drawing of the finished product and a space for a list of resources: 'You will need:' The format for the actual instructions will differ according to the needs of the children, but could include clues such as : 'What to do: 1st...... 2nd ....... 3rd ...... last.....'

## Making musical instruments

**Learning intention:** Knowledge and understanding of the world – to select the tools and techniques the children need to shape, assemble and join the materials they are using.

**Resources:** Assorted empty snack containers: biscuit and sweet tins, empty film canisters, small pebbles, rice, dried butter beans; milk bottle tops; conkers; paint and brushes; sticky paper; strong adhesive tape; assorted commercially produced shakers.

**What to do:** Explore the shakers together and discuss what makes the noise. Look at the reclaimed materials and discuss how shakers could be made. Encourage each child to choose a container to make a shaker. They can be simply made using small snack containers with tightly fitting lids. The children choose the contents of their shaker from the selection: a few conkers or pebbles or lots of rice or butter beans. Give the children plenty of opportunity to explore and discuss the natural objects and predict what sort of sound they will make in the shaker. Once the pot is full, seal it tightly with tape and encourage the children to paint it or decorate it with sticky paper. Filled film canisters make ideal tiny shakers and yoghurt pots can be covered as an alternative. When all the instruments are completed and dry, plan a music session with the home-made instruments accompanying favourite songs. Any children who have not chosen to make an instrument, but who want to join in, can use instruments from the music area.

- Plan a music session in which the adult plays a simple rhythm with a home-made percussion instrument for the children to play back. As they gain in confidence, individual children play their own rhythm for the others to repeat.

- Provide more resources and support children as they make their own drums and other percussion instruments.

- Provide pots, pans and dustbin lids with wooden spoons, outdoors, for children to make music on a larger scale.

## Salt dough biscuits and cakes

**Learning intention:** Physical – to handle tools, objects and malleable materials safely and with increasing control.

**Resources:** Salt dough recipe and ingredients (*Box 4.6*), assorted cutters including gingerbread men, bowls, wooden spoons, rolling pins, ready mixed paints, assorted brushes and PVA glue.

**What to do:** With the children mix the salt dough and knead until pliable. Encourage the children to roll out the dough and cut out biscuits and cakes. These should then be baked for at least 3 hours at 100°C (200°F/Gas Mark ¼). When the biscuits and cakes are fully dried out on both sides, turn off the oven and allow to cool.

When fully cool, investigate the cooked biscuits and cakes with the children and discuss the changes from the uncooked salt dough (keep one uncooked to observe). Give the children opportunities to paint and decorate the salt dough shapes in any way they wish. Finally seal the rock hard shapes with PVA glue and allow to dry.

---

## Box 4.6 Salt dough recipe

2 cups plain flour
1 cup salt
1 cup water
1 tablespoon lemon juice
1 tablespoon vegetable oil

Mix all ingredients together then knead until pliable

---

### Extensions

- Use the salt dough cakes and biscuits in a role play baker's shop or home corner.
- Use as props for the 'five currant buns' rhyme.
- Make other salt dough foods for role play.

## Moving like the animals

**Learning intention:** Physical development: to move with control and coordination.

**Resources:** Laminated A4 cards with pictures of animals, a washing line and pegs, a chalked track on the ground.

**What to do:** Either draw or stick one picture onto each A4 card. You can cut pictures from wrapping paper or use clip-art. Choose simple pictures to represent an elephant, a kangaroo, a rabbit and a small bird. Make sure there are several cards with the same picture on each. Fix the washing line somewhere safe in the outdoor area, slightly above child height. Peg the cards to the line to create a simple repeating pattern, for example, elephant, elephant, rabbit, rabbit, elephant, elephant, rabbit, rabbit. Gather the children together and look at and name the animals on the cards. Discuss the ways in which the creatures might move: perhaps huge, slow strides for the elephant, small hops for the rabbit, tiny pigeon steps for the bird and big jumps for the kangaroo. Give the children lots of time to practise moving around the chalked track in different ways. Encourage them to count their strides, jumps, pigeon steps and hops. Introduce the washing line with the picture patterns. Explain that the children need to follow the repeating pattern on the card as they move around the track: for example, two huge strides, two small hops, two huge strides, two small hops. When the children are confident with the pattern, create a new pattern together on the washing line. Then encourage the children to create patterns for each other.

## Extensions

- Give the children long, narrow pieces of card and lots of small clip-art pictures to create their own portable pattern cards.
- Play 'follow-the-leader' moving like different animals.

## The Nursery Band

**Learning intention:** Creative, to recognise and explore how sounds can be changed

**Resources:** A copy of the chant '*The Nursery Band*', seven assorted musical instruments in a basket.

Charlie's in the nursery band
Charlie's in the nursery band

The nursery
The nursery
Charlie's in the nursery band!

**What to do:** Introduce the chant to the children and practise it together. Discuss the musical instruments, how to play them and the sounds that they make. Form a circle with the children standing up and experiment with marching on the spot. Then ask the children to sit down, and place the basket of instruments in the centre of the circle.

Choose one child to be the leader of the nursery band. The child selects one instrument, and plays it while marching around the outside of the circle. All the other children chant 'the nursery band'. At the end of the verse, the leader of the band chooses another band member. This child selects an instrument and both children continue to march around the circle to the chant. Then a third child is chosen to join the band. This continues until all the instruments have gone.

## Extensions

- Introduce songs such as 'I am the music man and I come from down your way' and encourage the children to imitate the use of a wide range of musical instruments.
- Make a 'nursery band' number line with photos of the children playing the instruments.

## The importance of books and rhymes

Teachers need to provide a stimulating and challenging learning environment. This will support child-initiated learning and planning for adult-initiated activities and experiences across the six areas of learning. Daily group sessions should be planned to support children's communication, language and literacy development through books and rhymes.

## Core books

Teachers should consider developing the use of core books as these are an extremely effective way of supporting children's communication, language and literacy development.

Core books are, essentially, a selection of between twelve and twenty high quality texts which are used with children on a regular basis. The idea is that by the time they leave the nursery, the children will be very familiar with these books and will have developed a love of books. It is important to choose books by well-known and highly-regarded authors, as the children can then be introduced to books by the same author. To find out more about Core Books and Core Book lists go to: www.clpe. co.uk/publications/

Once the books have been identified, ensure that reference copies are available in the nursery, and that, where possible, multiple copies are purchased so that these can be loaned to families. Book packs are then developed for each core book. For example, a pack to support *We're Going on a Bear Hunt* could include a bear puppet and one to support *Handa's Surprise* could include a selection of plastic fruits.

## Possible core books

- *The Very Hungry Caterpillar* by Eric Carle
- *Handa's Surprise* by Eileen Browne
- *We're Going on a Bear Hunt* by Michael Rosen
- *Don't Put Your Finger in the Jelly, Nelly* by Nick Sharratt
- *Owl Babies* by Martin Waddell

- *This is the Bear* by Sarah Hayes
- *Once Upon a Time* by John Prater
- *So Much* by Trish Cooke
- *Give Me My Yam!* by Jan Blake
- *Where's My Teddy?* by Jez Alborough
- *Whatever Next!* by Jill Murphy
- *The Train Ride* by June Crebbin
- *Kipper* by Mick Inkpen
- *Dear Zoo* by Rod Campbell

## Story sacks

Teachers sometimes choose to develop story sacks to support core books. Story sacks are generally large cloth bags containing a good quality storybook with supporting materials such as puppets, soft toys, magnetic props, an information text and a game to support language activities. There is usually a story tape so that the children can follow along and act it out.

Story sacks are a popular, non-threatening way of encouraging families and the wider community to get involved in developing their own literacy and those of their children. If story sacks are developed for use at home, it is important to include a short guide containing questions to ask, words to consider and other ways of extending and sharing the book. To find out more about story sacks and suppliers go to: *www.standards.dfes.gov.uk/parentalinvolvement/pics/pics_storysacks www.storysack.com*

A story sack for *Handa's Surprise* could include:

- the book
- information text about fruit
- a set of magnetic story props
- fruit sorting counters

- fruit jigsaw puzzle
- plastic fruits
- recording of the story.

## Core rhymes

Staff teams in many nurseries identify core rhymes as well as books. These should be favourite rhymes and will often include rhymes which children bring from home to nursery. They will include traditional and contemporary rhymes as well as number rhymes (which are an essential way of developing children's understanding of number). The rhymes should be printed onto card and illustrated by the children. The cards should be laminated for durability, hole-punched and strung with bright cord or tape so that they can be hung on display.

Every week a core rhyme is chosen and chanted at group times. It will not be the only rhyme used during the week, but will give the children opportunities to either learn or revisit the words. Wherever possible, choose rhymes with actions as these will help the children to remember the rhymes. Rhymes are essential to children's communication, language and literacy development and provide a distinctive way of helping children to pay attention to and hear the sounds and rhythms of language. This attention to sounds provides the foundation for learning to read. Children cannot hear individual phonemes in words until they have had many opportunities to explore sound, rhythm and rhyme through rhythmic texts and rhymes.

Try to include Makaton signs with rhymes as this supports children experiencing language delay or disorder and may increase their confidence within the nursery. The signs used with rhymes are often very similar to the traditional actions and are easily learned by both adults and children.

Makaton Nursery Rhymes Video or DVD and other resources are available from: Makaton Vocabulary Development Project, www.makaton.org Tel: 01276 61390.

### Possible core rhymes

- *Five currant buns in a baker's shop*
- *Five little speckled frogs*
- *Ten in a bed*
- *Ten green bottles*
- *The wheels on the bus*
- *Twinkle, twinkle little star*
- *Tommy thumb*
- *I'm a little teapot*
- *Hickory, dickory dock*
- *Two little dicky birds*

# Magnetic props

It is important that children have access to props which help them to re-tell stories and rhymes. These can include objects such as a tea-set or plastic food, or soft toys and puppets to use as characters. Children can also be supported in re-telling favourite stories and rhymes through the use of magnetic props (*Box 4.7*). These are laminated coloured pictures which are used with magnetic boards or wedges. They give children opportunities to explore familiar rhymes and stories and make up their own. If the props are taken home, they can be used with a biscuit tin lid, metal tray or even the refrigerator door.

---

### Box 4.7 Making magnetic props

- choose a favourite book or rhyme
- identify characters and objects which are key to the rhyme or story
- draw the characters, initially in pencil and then fine black fibre pen
- photocopy the outline and keep a copy
- colour in the outline
- either scan the props, or have colour copies made, so that missing or damaged parts can be replaced later
- cut out the props and write the story or rhyme and number of pieces, in pencil, on the back, eg. 1/9, 2/9 and so on
- laminate the props and cut round each piece, leaving a border
- fix a small piece of magnetic rubber tape on the back (available from large stationers and educational catalogues, about £4 for a 10m roll).

# Setting challenges

It is important to support children as they follow their own play themes and to plan adult-initiated experiences which involve adult input. It is also important to offer children challenges throughout the nursery environment. Many nursery teachers also find that children respond to specific challenges which are set. These can be introduced to children at group times and will be based on children's interests and learning needs. Challenges can be set around any aspect of any of the six areas of learning. Although they may be aimed at certain groups of children, they need to be interesting enough and broad enough to engage all children. The general principle is for the teacher to set the challenge, establish a way of recording and then spend a short time later in the day discussing the outcomes with the children. Challenges will often follow on from an adult focus activity or something that the teacher has modelled. For example, if children have been learning a new number rhyme and the teacher has modelled the formation of the numeral '4', the challenge could be at some time during the session for children to have a go at writing the numeral 4 on a flip chart.

Children need time to become familiar with the idea of daily challenges, and in the early days may need lots of encouragement to become involved. Sometimes challenges will involve a time limit, or an amount of turns. Provide tocker timers, sand timers or another method to measure an approximate length of time. This could involve asking a friend to sing or chant one verse of a favourite song or rhyme, or running up and down the outdoor area a fixed number of times as the limit for completing a task. For example, a physical challenge could be to throw as many beanbags into a bucket or to jump up and down as many times as possible during the time it takes a friend to run around the playground. Remember to keep challenges simple at first, so that children feel able to have a go. As children gain in confidence, encourage them to think of challenges for each other. Consider involving families in weekend or half-term challenges such as fitting as many objects as possible into a film canister or collecting as many different leaves as possible.

## Possible challenges

### Personal, Social and Emotional Development

- Find out the name of an unfamiliar child and be able to say it at group time (good for the beginning of term).
- Do up as many buttons as possible before the timer runs out, then undo them again.
- Think of one thing they like to do at home and be prepared to talk about it.
- Draw a picture of one friend who is happy.
- Make a sign to depict an agreed shared boundary – 'no running indoors', 'no dog in the playground', 'share with friends'.
- Ask one friend to play a known game such as 'row, row, row your boat'.
- Ask one friend to share a cooperative wheeled toy outdoors.

### Communication, Language and Literacy

- Find out, by talking to others, as many words as possible which mean the same as a given word, e.g. 'enormous' (gigantic, huge, vast, mammoth, massive) and feed back verbally in discussion.
- Find an object beginning with a particular initial letter from round the room and place it in the basket.
- Find an object which rhymes with another object from around the room and place it in the basket. The object could be a lock (wok, rock, sock, clock, block) or a log (frog, cog, dog, hog).

- Have a go at writing a specific letter on a flip chart.
- Have a go at writing your name on a sticky label and wearing it.
- Find a book about a particular topic, eg. bears, cars or dinosaurs.
- Choose a favourite rhyme, write and/or draw a clue to help others to guess which one it is.

### Mathematical Development

- Guess the number of objects in a box and record the number in any way.
- Choose an envelope, put a specific number of objects in, and record the contents, in any way, on the outside.
- Make a price label for an item of shopping.
- Count the number of coins in a Chinese New Year envelope.
- Feel three boxes and decide which is the heaviest. Make a mark to indicate choice.
- Find an item of a specific two-dimensional or three-dimensional shape, and place it in a basket.
- Look at the contents of three clear containers, decide which has the most and which has the least, put your name card under the container.
- Find the smallest or largest leaf possible.
- Grab as many sorting objects from a basket with one hand, count and place them on own name card.

### Knowledge and Understanding of the World

- Think of one question to ask a class soft toy or puppet about a specific topic. Bertie the Bear has been shopping, think of a question to ask him about his trip.
- Find something which meets a specific criterion – soft, stretchy, shiny, hard, sticky, stripy, furry, bouncy.

- Design and make a house for a compare bear (or soft toy, puppet or plastic person).
- Move a programmable toy from one place to another on a floor plan.
- Use a recorder to record a favourite rhyme onto a cassette.
- Find out something about a living thing and record it through any form of mark-making or drawing – tadpoles, mini-beasts, fish, runner beans, amaryllis.
- Select one object in a feely box, try to guess what it is, tell a friend, then check to find out. Or see how many objects are correctly guessed from a set number.
- Smell contents of three containers, record guesses about contents, using ticks or crosses against photographs.

## Physical Development

- Two people together throw and catch a ball and count – see which pair can do the most without dropping.
- Throw ten beanbags into a bucket, record how many hit the target.
- Find one way to make a loud noise using just body parts.
- Move as many objects as possible from one basket to another, using tweezers or chopsticks, until the timer stops.
- Make a very long snake from playdough or Plasticene.
- Make as long a necklace as possible by threading beads until the timer finishes – put it with your name card.
- Find a beanbag with your name on, throw it as far as possible from a given spot – see who throws the furthest.
- Use a magnet to catch as many fish as possible before the timer finishes.

## Creative Development

- Colour mix to match a specific shade, put a thumbprint of colour on a name label.

- Draw a picture of a favourite thing in one square on a huge group piece of paper.
- Find something outdoors with an interesting texture and fix it to a collaborative collage.
- Use a percussion instrument to create a rhythm and record it.
- Draw a picture, or make marks to represent a storyline which includes plastic animals, vehicles and people. Place the picture on a huge piece of paper on a table.
- Play with a bear and a rucksack, which contains a toothbrush, comb and swimming trunks and tell a friend what the bear has been doing and where he has been.
- Make up a dance or a way of moving to match a piece of music – share it later with the group.

---

### Handy Hints

- Successful, effective teachers plan for adult-initiated activities and encourage, support and extend child-initiated experiences.
- Core provision allows children to access the same high-quality resources every day in provision areas. Provision should be enhanced to meet children's learning needs and interests.
- A variety of trays can be used to present malleable, tactile, exploratory and imaginative experiences in exciting and creative ways.
- When planning adult focus activities, identify one clear learning intention linked to the stepping stones for one of the six areas of learning.
- Develop core books and rhymes with props to support children's communication, language and literacy development.
- Encourage children to engage in challenges which inspire them to try new activities and experiences.

CHAPTER 5

# WORKING WITH COLLEAGUES AND PARENTS OR CARERS

## INTRODUCTION

The number of adults working in even a one form entry primary school seems to have blossomed over the last two decades. Where once the staff team would have included possibly seven teachers, a head teacher, nursery nurse, one or two classroom assistants (probably called primary helpers), a secretary, premises officer (or caretaker) and school meals staff, now sometimes in excess of forty people are employed. Responsibilities have changed and teachers are often leading large, diverse teams. Nursery teachers may or may not be responsible for leading the whole foundation stage team, which will include all nursery and reception classes. But a nursery teacher will be the leader of a team, however small. At a bare minimum, the nursery team will consist of the nursery teacher and a nursery nurse with a qualification in childcare (generally a NVQ (National Vocational Qualification) level 3, NNEB (Nursery Nurse Examinations Board) or BTec (Business and Technical Education Council)), with 25 or 26 children. However, teachers are now often working in integrated early years settings as well as in schools, and a larger team could include:

- reception teachers
- nursery nurses in nursery and reception classes
- teaching assistants
- meals supervisors

- bi-lingual assistants
- teaching support for children with English as an additional language
- learning mentors
- students
- health professionals.

When working in a team, it is essential that every team member has clear roles and responsibilities and that everyone is aware of each member's duties. This chapter will include some consideration of:

- roles and responsibilities
- working with colleagues
- working with parents or carers.

## THE NURSERY TEAM

### Adults working together in the nursery need

- a shared understanding of the aims and philosophy of early years education
- knowledge and understanding of the needs and characteristics of young children
- knowledge of child development and clear and appropriate expectations of children at different ages and stages
- a clear understanding of how children learn through play and the provision necessary to ensure high quality experiences
- a genuine interest in and sensitivity towards children

- to provide a welcoming, stimulating environment which allows all children to feel secure and valued
- to work in partnership with parents and carers, and have an understanding of the crucial role of parents as children's first educators
- to evaluate their own attitudes about gender, race, culture and disability
- to be familiar with and implement all policies
- a shared sense of purpose and a vision for the future
- good working relationships based on mutual respect, trust and support
- confidence to try out new ideas without fear of failure
- a clear understanding of their own roles and responsibilities and those of others
- effective skills and strategies which ensure good communication
- the ability to be flexible and adaptable in their approach
- to develop effective strategies for observing and record-keeping
- opportunities to plan, monitor and evaluate their provision and practice
- skills in planning and implementing an effective, developmentally appropriate, early years curriculum
- opportunities to reflect upon their own practice and develop their skills, knowledge and understanding
- an understanding of the importance of providing good role models for children and colleagues
- to develop support networks with other professionals, establishments and other agencies
- to be aware of current thinking and developments in the field of early years education through reading and attending courses and conferences

- a view of themselves as learners and an understanding of the importance of ongoing training and professional development.

From *Learning for Life, a Curriculum for the Early Years* (LEARN, 2000)

## Leading the nursery team

It is a question that is often asked: 'are leaders born or made?'. Whatever the answer, there are key elements which the teacher leading a nursery team needs to consider. It may be quite challenging for a young or inexperienced teacher to suddenly become the leader of a team, particularly if the other team members are more experienced or older. Teachers who take the time to chat to any member of a nursery team will hear stories of enthusiastic young teachers who have swept in with lots of bright (and genuinely sound) ideas, to have been met with antagonism or apathy. Nursery teachers need to remember that they may be the team leader, but they must also be a team player and that the first task of developing a new team is to ensure all team members have shared understandings. A good starting point could be to share the list above and have a frank discussion about the content. Every team member could spend some time considering the points and rate them from one to five on a scale that goes from '1 – strongly agree' to '5 – strongly disagree'. The team could develop a new list which includes everything they subscribe to, including their own additions.

The nursery teacher, as team leader, will have specific tasks which will include:

- ensuring effective communication within the team and into the wider community
- deciding on priorities, based on team discussions

- ensuring all team members feel valued by utilising all skills and qualities of individuals and developing an effective team approach
- overall responsibility for the monitoring of planning and record-keeping
- identifying the professional development needs of the team and ensuring that these are met.

Some nursery teachers also have a middle or senior management role within the school and may have the position of foundation stage or early years coordinator or leader. The job descriptions for these posts vary enormously but generally include responsibility for the leadership and management of the foundation stage as a whole, and transition from home to nursery and into key stage 1. It is important that foundation stage leaders are very clear about their additional roles and responsibilities and develop good working relationships with other key stage leaders.

## Working with parents or carers

The *Curriculum guidance for the foundation stage* emphasises the importance of parents or carers and practitioners working together to impact positively on children's learning.

A successful partnership needs a two-way flow of information, knowledge and expertise. There are many ways of achieving partnership with parents or carers, but the following are common features of effective practice:

- the past and future part played by parents or carers in the education of their children is recognised and explicitly encouraged

- practitioners show respect and understanding for the role of the parents or carers in their child's education
- practitioners listen to parents' or carers' accounts of their children's development and any concerns they have
- arrangements for settling in are flexible enough to give time for children to become secure and for practitioners and parents or carers to discuss each child's circumstances, interests, skills and needs
- all parents or carers are made to feel welcome, valued and necessary through a range of different opportunities for collaboration between children, parents or carers and practitioners
- the knowledge and expertise of parents and other family adults are used to support the learning opportunities provided by the setting
- practitioners use a variety of ways to keep parents or carers fully informed about the curriculum, such as brochures, displays and videos which are available in the home languages of the parents, and through informal discussions
- parents or carers and practitioners talk about and record information about the child's progress and achievements, for example through making a book about the child
- relevant learning activities and play activities, such as reading and sharing books, are continued at home. Similarly, experiences at home are used to develop learning in the setting, for example visits and celebrations.

*Curriculum guidance for the foundation stage*
(QCA, 2000)

## Home visits

Schools and other early years settings have very different policies about home visiting and settling children into nursery. These very first contacts are the most important as they can set the scene for future relationships.

Home visits are often seen as very beneficial as they give teachers and other nursery team members opportunities to meet children and their families in their own homes, where they feel most comfortable. I have often been reminded about individual children's experiences: 'You know, when you were at my house, that box, you remember...'. Many schools choose to offer home visits to those families who want them. Visits may be seen as intrusive, particularly by families who may have to allow unwelcome professionals into their homes. When home visits are introduced, the take-up can initially be quite low. But if schools and families are absolutely clear about the purpose of the visit and the benefits for the child, word-of-mouth is a very effective means of ensuring a better take-up every term.

Home visits can take many forms, but there are several criteria which should be applied universally.

- Set up an agreed date and time in advance and stick to the time

- Always allow plenty of travelling time between visits.

- Be very clear about the length and content of the visit – it is a good time to fill in the first page of the individual child profile.

- Never visit alone. Ensure one member of staff talks to the parent(s) or carer(s) and the other spends time with the child.

- Develop a special visit bag with selected books and activities such as a simple puzzle, or construction equipment. Make sure these resources are available at nursery during the settling-in period.

- Decide what refreshments you will accept if offered, and be consistent or risk causing offence. A non-alcoholic drink is usually acceptable, a full meal is generally inadvisable.

■ If the child will have a book bag in the nursery, consider leaving it at the home visit.

## Settling in

Whether a home visit is carried out or not, the settling-in period can be a very useful time for getting to know children and their families. Ensure there is a clear settling-in policy which outlines the procedures. Stagger starting dates so that just a few children start during each session. This allows parents to stay and see how the nursery operates. Consider making the first few days each child attends a short session, so that new children arrive a little late and leave before tidying up begins. This means they can avoid the hustle and bustle which can be quite unsettling for the uninitiated.

Many teachers organise an open meeting during the first week of term for the families of all children starting in the nursery that term. A supply teacher covers the teacher role during the meeting, so that the parents or carers have an opportunity to meet each other, hear a little about the nursery, see how it operates and then join in a few activities with their offspring. Keep the visit short, but informative to encourage families to stay again.

## Sharing skills and expertise

Many teachers invite family members to help in the nursery. This gives parents or carers opportunities to share their skills and expertise. It also offers children opportunities to interact with even more interesting adults. To make sure there are no misunderstandings, confirm that appropriate police checks have been carried out if necessary, and that induction arrangements are in place. Family members need to understand and adhere to school policies and procedures and to be aware of confidentiality issues. Some parents or carers will need more support than others to feel confident working with children, and it is often these adults who have the most to offer. Make sure that everyone is clear about what the parent's or carer's role is in the class during each visit, so that it is a mutually beneficial, successful event.

Many families may not be able, or wish, to spend time in the nursery but they can contribute in other ways. Take some time to find out their talents, and utilise these. Seek out people who may be willing to record stories in home languages, write notices in different scripts, loan favourite music CDs, pictures or artefacts for displays. Remember to include all families when making collections of free resources (see *Chapter 3*).

## Sharing the curriculum

Teachers sometimes feel that families do not support children's learning at home. Families sometimes feel that their children spend all their time at nursery running around, getting messy or just playing. These attitudes stem from a lack of communication and understanding. Teachers need to offer families opportunities to find out more about the curriculum and how children learn. This can be done in a number of ways, some of which will be more appropriate for some families than for others:

- Displays about aspects of the curriculum which include lots of photographs and examples of children's achievements
  - what we learn outdoors
  - how we learn to write
  - why physical development is so important
  - all about messy play.
- A nursery brochure with lots of photographs, giving clear information about practical issues such as appropriate

clothing, starting and finishing times and how children learn through play.

■ Workshops about aspects of the curriculum which include ideas for supporting children at home, for example through practical maths or sharing books and story props.

■ Informal discussions about what children have done during the session, and what they have learned.

## Sharing children's achievements

Whether the first page of the individual child profile is completed during the home visit, a meeting or the child's first session in nursery, it is the opening chapter in the ongoing dialogue between home and nursery and is vital to every child's success. Teachers must plan regular, structured meetings during which parents or carers and practitioners share information about children's achievements in the nursery and at home. These meetings should be in addition to informal meetings which may be arranged if parents or carers have a concern about their child.

Nurseries have varying policies regarding written statements about children's achievements. Some provide termly or annual written feedback, while others choose to produce a written summary only at the end of the child's nursery career, as they move into the reception year.

A written summary of each child's achievements, based on the individual child profile, should be discussed with parents or carers and wherever possible, should include a parental contribution. This summary should include all six areas of learning, emphasising the child's strengths and also possible next steps for learning. Copies of the summary should be given to the parents or carers and also passed on to the next teacher. See *A Focus on Planning* (LEARN, 2004) for photocopiable formats and more guidance.

### Handy Hints

- Practitioners in the nursery team need to be clear about their roles and responsibilities.
- All nursery teachers lead a nursery team, however small, and need to develop appropriate leadership strategies.
- The *Curriculum guidance for the foundation stage* emphasises the importance of parents or carers and practitioners working together to impact positively on children's learning.

## CHAPTER 6

# LOOKING AFTER YOURSELF

## INTRODUCTION

Professional working people need time away from their work so that they can relax, clear their minds and recover from the stresses and strains of work. It is important that you find time to look after yourself.

## WORK–LIFE BALANCE

The Workload Agreement (www.teachernet.gov.uk/wholeschool/remodelling) signed by the government, employers and unions in January 2003, and now effective in law, gave teachers the right to a better work–life balance. The expression 'work–life balance' has emerged over the past 10 years as employers have realised that spending more and more hours at work is not necessarily a good thing and does not equate to greater productivity. Indeed, it can lead to burn-out, apathy and antipathy to work. The work–life balance aims to help teachers avoid stress, anxiety and depression and maintain the high self-esteem that is a prerequisite for good teaching. The Workload Agreement is beneficial for teachers and identifies many administrative and clerical tasks which should now be undertaken by administrators and classroom assistants, rather than teachers.

# STRESS

A totally stress-free life is neither possible nor desirable. Limited acute stress, brought on by events such as competitive sport, family occasions and dangerous situations (or writing a book) can actually strengthen the immune system. We are all aware that persistent stress can cause damage to physical and psychological health. But many people think that 'stress' is an overused term, and when we are stressed, it can sometimes be so much of a way of life that it becomes hard to identify.

The American Psychological Association (APA; www.apa.org) has identified a number of symptoms of stress, which include:

- headaches
- stomach upsets – indigestion, nausea, diarrhoea
- increased skin problems
- shortness of breath
- insomnia
- fatigue
- mood swings
- irritability or anxiety
- depression
- loss of sense of humour
- nervousness
- forgetfulness
- lacking concentration
- disorganisation
- apathy
- negative self-perception.

If you are experiencing a number of these symptoms, you should consider whether you are stressed. Of course you know yourself best, and it is worth considering changes in behaviour or the way you feel. It's no good blaming your headache, stomach upset and tiredness on stress if you've just had one of those overly indulgent weekends and left it too late to get up on a Monday morning.

## Managing stress

It is really important to look at ways of managing the pressures which lead to stress.

One of the huge disadvantages of modern living is the non-stop communication explosion. We sometimes feel we are at everyone's beck and call, all day and all night. It is important that on some evenings and weekends we are not available. Consider turning off the laptop and mobile phone and make sure you keep some time for yourself. It is essential to find time, at least once a week, to do something you enjoy. It could be an regular evening class or, just as usefully, a more flexible arrangement which could include time to read a novel, go to a show, disappear into the greenhouse or find time to enjoy yourself and laugh with friends. I know it isn't easy to do. As a busy teacher with a young family, I never seemed to find 'me time'. In fact, when I finally did sign up to a pottery evening class, it was such a unique event that it was recorded in my 6-year-old son's writing about his family: 'and my mummy likes to go out in the evenings'.

## Exercise

Of course exercise helps the brain to function better, and keeping the heart and circulation primed helps us respond under pressure. It's really important to do at least 20 minutes of aerobic exercise at least three times a week. An hour a week can sound a lot, but it doesn't necessarily mean a trip to the gym, or purchasing a cycling or running machine (particularly as these are often ignored after the first flush of enthusiasm). But 20 minutes of even-paced, brisk walking is likely to be just as effective, and more sustainable, especially in good company. If all this seems too much, consider wearing a pedometer to see just how many steps you walk in a day. It is recommended that we all walk 10 000 steps daily to keep fit, but our increasingly sedentary lives often lead to far less.

## Diet

It may sound boring, but a healthy diet is also a great stress-beater. Good nutrition keeps body and mind in top condition, and more prepared to cope with pressure. B vitamins are vital for a healthy nervous system and sustained energy. Nutrients absorbed through food are generally more effective than any vitamin supplement, so it's important to include fresh green vegetables, fish, poultry, whole grains, pulses and bananas as part of daily diet.

# High blood pressure

Stress can also contribute to high blood pressure, of which sufferers are often unaware. It is really important to monitor your own general health. More than one-third of adults in the UK have high blood pressure. Simple changes can reduce risk dramatically, and cutting down on salt intake can cause huge benefits. Of course, we all need some salt; it is crucial for nutrient absorption and helps to maintain normal blood pressure. It is often not enough simply to cut down on salt at the table. Many ready meals (including the so-called healthy options) are full of added salt. In fact, the salt content in low-fat, low-sugar, low-calorie ready meals is often far higher than in normal meals, in order to add taste. It's worth checking labels, but remember to check for different words for salt, such as sodium or sodium chloride.

As well as reducing salt, there are other important factors to remember to keep high blood pressure under control:

- take that 20 minutes exercise, three times a week
- try to keep to your ideal weight
- monitor fat intake
- don't smoke
- have regular blood pressure checks.

# Time management

One of the biggest challenges every nursery teacher faces is that there are never enough hours in the day. It is therefore essential to develop effective strategies to prioritise what is important and what can wait.

One effective way is to consider the bigger picture and break this down into bite-sized, achievable pieces. As every task is accomplished, it can be highlighted. This will give a sense of achievement to individuals and to the team. The identification of small tasks ensures that tasks appear more manageable, and attainments can be celebrated. This gives a more positive and realistic picture than one clouded by the enormity of the tasks left to do.

If one major priority is the development of resources, a long-term objective could be 'to develop appropriate resources to support all areas of provision, indoors and outdoors', and tasks could be identified as follows:

### Year 1, term 1

1.  Develop book and graphics areas
    *   audit present resources
    *   find out more about LEA loans scheme
    *   arrange to visit local nursery class noted for excellent communication, language and literacy provision
    *   list resources needed, in order of priority
    *   discuss books with language coordinator
    *   order Core Books list
    *   make list of free items and begin to collect from children's families and friends.
2.  Join *Early Years Outdoors* organisation.
3.  Subscribe to *Early Years Educator (EYE)* magazine.
4.  Investigate possible funding for developing outdoors area.
5.  Contact Learning through Landscapes, an organisation which offers support and advice on ways to maximise outdoor spaces (www.ltl.org.uk).
6.  Visit three nearby schools with recommended outdoor areas.

7.  Discuss proposed developments with LEA Early Years Adviser and seek advice.

### Year 1, term 2

1.  Order and oversee construction and development of outdoor playhouse.
2.  Develop home corner role play.
    (Break these down into bite-sized pieces.)

### Year 1, term 3

1.  Develop role-play boxes for two scenarios.
2.  Plan playground markings with children and oversee working group from local secondary school to mark out tarmac area.

In addition to these planned developments, numerous tasks will arise on a day-to-day basis which will need to be dealt with. It is important to have an efficient system to deal with these issues. There are many different ways of ensuring that everything is accomplished, but a notebook is always a good idea. Try noting everything down on an ongoing list, as it arises, giving it a priority number:

1.  Do this as soon as possible today.
2.  Deal with this by the end of the week.
3.  Build this into the longer term plan.
4.  Delegate this to........

Cross out or highlight every item as it is achieved, and ensure that the most important things are dealt with in order of priority.

# TIME-SAVING STRATEGIES

In order to save time in the long term, it is often necessary to invest time initially. It is well worth the effort of putting effective systems in place to ensure that the level of maintenance needed for the day-to-day running of the nursery is minimised. Consider:

## The organisation of the learning environment

Ensure that all areas of provision and storage are clearly labelled with words and pictures so that adults and children know where resources are stored. Involve children in the tidying up process. This is a great way of developing their independence and autonomy and of giving them opportunities to sort in meaningful situations. Young children can be responsible for washing equipment, scrubbing painty surfaces, sweeping up and returning resources to the correct places. They will need lots of support in the early days, and adults may feel it is quicker to just do it themselves. But persevere. After a while children will begin to organise tidying up themselves and this means less teacher-time spent at the sink or fixing puzzle pieces. Develop a nursery culture of never putting away incomplete equipment, puzzles, games or kits. This reduces time spent later searching for missing parts. Have a wicker basket for odd bits which are found. Make sure this is emptied and the parts are returned to the correct place at least weekly.

## Team meetings

Time is precious, don't waste it. Have a central staff board where key information is displayed so discussion time isn't lost. If there are decisions to be made, or if there is lots of information to share, give out information before the meeting so that all the team can come prepared and informed. Always have a clear agenda, with timings. At the beginning of the meeting appoint a time-keeper and a minute-taker (take turns at this) and ensure that you adhere to the times set.

## Systems of communication

Have a shared staff message board where all the team write important messages, to reduce the time spent transmitting information. This can include messages about resources needed or non-confidential information about children or families, such as early pick ups, illness, or details of a change in who is collecting an individual child.

## Planning and record-keeping

Spend some time identifying the learning which can take place across the six areas throughout the provision. Create a clear overview of the knowledge and understanding, skills and attitudes which can be developed in each area. Add one or two photographs on an A3 sheet, laminate and display in each area of provision. This saves time spent on short-term planning, as possible learning intentions for child-initiated activities do not have to be identified again in the weekly or daily plans.

At the start of each term, identify the vocabulary which is likely to be introduced or reinforced throughout the environment. Print out each word and laminate. Use sock dryers (the round mobiles with pegs attached, often used when camping) to display the key vocabulary in the appropriate areas of provision each week. This means weekly vocabulary doesn't have to be repeated on plans.

Fix actual observations into individual child profiles – it isn't necessary to copy these out, as the profiles are working documents.

# MAKING THE MOST OF THE LONG HOLIDAYS

One of the great benefits of teaching as a profession is the holidays. You may choose to spend some time catching up on paperwork or preparing for the next term, but there is still a lot of free time within the 13 weeks' break, particularly in comparison to other professions, which may be limited to 4 or 5 weeks' time off plus bank holidays.

Of course, there are always the usual package trips, but sometimes it's worth considering something different in the quest to unwind and recharge the batteries.

## Home swaps

Consider swapping your home for a couple of weeks with a comparable property in Europe, Australia or America. For an annual fee and the cost of the airfare, you can have a very economic base from which to explore a whole new country. In general, companies provide a service in which your details are listed on their website, and they provide advice and support for the home swap holiday.

- Homelink International (Tel: 01962 886 882, www. homelink.org.uk)
- Exchanges Worldwide (www.exchangesworldwide.com)
- Home Exchange Network (Tel: 0141 571 8068, www.home-exchange-network.com)

## Working holiday as a volunteer

You can work as a volunteer, assisting scientists on dozens of environmental projects around the world, from Alaska to Vietnam. Alternatively, do something worthwhile nearer home and volunteer to work at one of the hundreds of National Trust sites around the country.

- Earthwatch (Tel: 01865 318 838, www.earthwatch.org)
- Discovery Initiatives (Tel: 01285 643 333, www. discoveryinitiatives.com)
- National Trust (Tel: 0870 458 4000, www.nationaltrust.org.uk)

## On a budget

Consider a multi-activity break with canoeing, caving, climbing and abseiling, staying in a youth hostel. Stay at the Edale Activity Centre in Derbyshire's Peak National Park for less than £15 a night. Or try rock climbing, ghyll scrambling, fell walking, kayaking or exploring the ravines and waterfalls of the Lakeland ghylls of Lake Windermere in Cumbria, or any of the other great locations across the UK.

- Y.H.A. (Tel: 08700 770 8868, www.yha.org.uk)

## A change is as good as a rest

### Teaching exchange

There really is something to the old saying 'a change is as good as a rest'. If you are a new graduate interested in developing your teaching skills abroad, or an experienced teacher looking for a new challenge, consider a teaching exchange through the British Council. Teachers in the UK can swap places with a colleague in the United States through the Fulbright programme. The exchange can last 3–6 weeks, the autumn term or a whole year. Your full teaching salary is transferable and the British Council provides a grant to cover travel costs. Applications must be made by January for exchanges commencing in the autumn of the same year.

## Overseas study trip

If the thought of a teacher exchange sounds too daunting, you may prefer an in-service overseas study visit. The Teachers' International Professional programme (TIPD) enables teachers from England to experience good educational practice in different countries around the world. The programme is funded by the DfES and the Department for International Development (DFID). To find out more, visit www.britishcouncil.org.

# If it all gets too much

The Teacher Support Network is a national, independent charity that offers free services to improve the wellbeing and effectiveness of all teachers. This includes personalised, practical and emotional support online as well as resources and guides on issues including work–life balance, stress management and pupil behaviour.

The Teacher Support Line offers confidential, solution-focused support, 24 hours a day, 365 days a year, from trained counsellors who all have experience of education (www.teachersupport.info, Tel: 08000 562 561).

## Handy Hints

- A work-life balance aims to help teachers avoid stress, anxiety and depression and to maintain the high self-esteem that is a pre-requisite for good teaching.
- Be aware of the symptoms of stress and how it can be managed.
- Find time for yourself and develop an outlet away from work.
- Develop your time management skills and prioritise effectively.
- Use the school holidays to the greatest advantage.
- Consider an overseas study trip or teaching exchange to develop your expertise.
- If it all gets too much, and colleagues and friends can't help, seek confidential, professional support.

# BIBLIOGRAPHY

## REFERENCES

Department for Education and Skills (2004) *Every Child Matters: Next Steps.* DfES Publications, Nottingham www.everychildmatters.gov.uk

Department for Education and Skills (2005) *Key Elements of Effective Practice (KEEP).* Ref: DfES 1201-2005G. DfES Publications, Nottingham www.standards.dfes.gov.uk

Dowling M (2005) *Supporting Young Children's Sustained Shared Thinking.* Early Education, London

Effective Provision of Pre-school Education (EPPE) (2003) *Intensive Case Studies of Practice across the Foundation Stage.* Technical Paper 10 - The EPPE Project. DfES/Institute of Education, London

Lewisham Early Years Advice and Resource Network (2000) *Learning for Life. A Curriculum for the Early Years.* 2nd edn. London Borough of Lewisham, London

Lewisham Early Years Advice and Resource Network (2004) *Focus on Planning – Effective Planning and Assessment in the Foundation Stage.* London Borough of Lewisham, London

Lindon J (1993) *Child Development from Birth to Eight.* National Children's Bureau, London

Moyles J, Adams S, Musgrove A (2002) *SPEEL – Study of Pedagogical Effectiveness in Early Years.* DfES, London

Qualifications and Curriculum Authority (2000) *Curriculum guidance for the foundation stage.* Ref: QCA/00/587. QCA Publications, Norwich www.qca.org.uk

Qualifications and Curriculum Authority (2001) *Planning for Learning in the Foundation Stage.* QCA Publications, Norwich www.qca.org.uk

Qualifications and Curriculum Authority (2003) *Foundation Stage Profile Handbook.* Ref: QCA/03/1006. QCA Publications, Norwich www.qca.org.uk

Qualifications and Curriculum Authority (2005) *Seeing steps in children's learning.* (DVD and guide) Ref: QCA/05/1546. QCA Publications, Norwich www.qca.org.uk

## FURTHER READING

Adair J (1986) *Effective Teambuilding.* Pan Books, London

Ashman C, Green S (2004) *Managing People and Teams.* David Fulton, London

Bayley R, Broadbent L (2001) *50 Exciting Things to do Outside.* Lawrence Educational Publications, Walsall

Bilton H (2002) *Outdoor Play in the Early Years.* 2nd edn. David Fulton, London

Bruce T (2001) *Learning through Play.* Hodder and Stoughton, London

Bubb S, Earley P (2004), *Managing Teacher Workload: Work-life Balance and Well-being.* Paul Chapman, London

Crawford M, Kydd L, Riches D (1997) *Leadership and Teams in Educational Management.* Open University Press, Buckingham

Department for Education and Skills (2004) *Parents: Partners in Learning.* DfES Publications, Nottingham www.standards. dfes.gov.uk/primary/publications/literacy/1092095/

Edgington M (2002) *The Great Outdoors.* Early Education, London

Edgington M (2004) *The Foundation Stage Teacher in Action – Teaching 3, 4 and 5 year olds.* 3rd edn. Paul Chapman Publishing, London

Ellis S, Barrs M (1996) *The Core Book.* CLPE, London

Hall N, Robinson A (2003) *Exploring Writing and Play in the Early Years.* 2nd edn. David Fulton, London

Jefferson A, Hunter F (2005) *High Blood Pressure - Food, Facts and Recipes.* Hamlyn, London

Kenway P (1995) *Working with Parents.* Save the Children, London

Lazim A (2005) *The Core Book List.* CLPE, London

Lewisham Early Years Advice and Resource Network (2002) *A Place to Learn.* London Borough of Lewisham, London

Lindon J (2001) *Understanding Children's Play.* Nelson Thornes, London

Meggitt C, Sunderland G (2000) *Child Development: An Illustrated Guide.* Heinemann, Oxford

Nutbrown C (1994) *Threads of Thinking: Young Children Learning and the Role of Early Education.* Paul Chapman, London

Ouvry M (2000) *Exercising Muscles and Minds.* The National Early Years Network, London

Pound L (1999) *Supporting Mathematical development in the Early Years.* Open University Press, Buckingham

Rodd J (1998) *Leadership in Early Childhood.* 2nd edn. Open University Press, Buckingham

Siraj-Blatchford J, MacLeod-Brudenell I (1999) *Supporting Science, Design and Technology in the Early Years.* Open University Press, Buckingham

Whalley M, and the Penn Green Centre Team (2001) *Involving Parents in their Children's Learning.* Paul Chapman, London

Whalley M (2004) *Management in Early Childhood Settings.* Paul Chapman, London

# USEFUL WEBSITES

All websites were accessed in February 2006.

The following websites contain a wealth of information about current national initiatives in the foundation stage, and are worth exploring as they are frequently updated:

**www.everychildmatters.gov.uk**
Includes lots of downloads of current documents about childcare and education and links to other relevant sites.

**www.teachernet.gov.uk**
Almost everything you need to know about professional development and educational research. Also has information about Teachers TV.

**www.surestart.gov.uk**
Regular newsletters and downloads to keep practitioners up to date with current early years initiatives.

**www.standards.dfes.gov.uk/primary/**
Lots of information about the Foundation Stage Profile, Foundation Stage Units, KEEP and raising standards in the Foundation stage.

**www.qca.org.uk**
Download or order all QCA publications from this site.

**www.surestart.gov.uk/research/keyreseach/eppe**
Includes the main findings and the whole report of the Effective Provision of Pre-school Education (EPPE) research.

**www.dfes.gov.uk/rsgateway/DB/RRP/u013617/index.shtml**
Includes information about the Study of Pedagogical Effectiveness in Early Learning (SPEEL)

The following websites contain information about specific topics mentioned in the text:

**www.principlesintopractice.org**
The Principles into Practice website includes a web-tool which practitioners in each early years setting can access via a password. This allows the whole staff team to monitor their progress on a regular basis.

**www.britishcouncil.org**
Information about teacher exchanges overseas.

**www.fulbright.co.uk**
Information about teacher exchanges to the United States.

**www.domestic-waterfowl.co.uk**
The site to visit if considering rearing ducks or chickens in school.

**www.clpe.co.uk/publications**
Core books lists and lots more.

**www.insectlore.co.uk**
Suppliers of live butterfly kits, silkworms and anything else to do with mini-beasts.

**www.rspca.org.uk**
This site gives lots of sound, practical advice about caring for pets.

**www.ltl.org.uk**
Learning through Landscapes is an organisation which offers support and advice on ways to maximise outdoor spaces.

# ADDITIONAL RESOURCES

Not sure where to get some of the items mentioned? These suppliers have some great ideas for resources to stimulate and inspire adults and children alike. All websites were accessed and telephone numbers checked in February 2006.

## Early Steps (TTS Group)

TTS supply a wide range of unusual and interesting resources including:

- The TUFF Spot – a large, flexible black tray, which can be used indoors or outdoors, originally designed for mixing concrete
- Mirrored tuff spot – a safe, plastic mirror which gives the original tuff spot a whole new range of features.
- Pea gravel, bark chippings, moonglow gravel, coloured gravel, moonstone black pebbles, black shimmer sand, alphabet noodles, loose rock packs, dried pulses, gem stones, natural sponges, abalone shells, glass stones, feathers – for exploratory or imaginative play.
- Natural fibre matting, landscape matting (looks like grass), iridescent shred, silver foil blankets, decorative net – to enhance imaginative or role play or for display.

- Instant snow powder - when the real thing just isn't available. Add water and create two gallons of non-toxic, fluffy snow.
- Squidgy sparkling numbers.
- Bubble bonanza – very good for blowing bubbles.
- Sculpting sand - turns into putty in water and can be sculpted. Turns back into dry sand when removed.
- Hypo-allergenic shaving foam and bulk quantities of food essence, food colouring and cornflour.
- Bee-bot programmable toy.

**www.tts-group.co.uk.**
**Tel:01623 447 800.**

## Mindstretchers

Mindstretchers supply a range of unusual resources to support exploratory and imaginative play, with an emphasis on outdoor play, including:

- waterproof or glitzy child size butterfly wings
- collections to explore and sort – spoons, hearts and others
- number confetti
- organza bags felt bags and miniature baskets
- wooden ladybirds and plastic mice and rats
- acrylic gemstones
- collapsible bucket and water barrel

**www.mindstretchers.co.uk.**
**Tel: 01764 664409.**

# Lawrence Educational

Lawrence Educational supply exciting and innovative resources for early years practitioners – books, CDs, videos and puppets, including:

- the '*Dogum*' series to support speaking, listening and thinking
- the '*Helping Young Children Series*' – which focuses on aspects of learning
- *Beat Babies* and books
- Ros Bayley's '*Really rhythmic raps*' series
- *50 exciting ideas* series, which includes Storylines – ideas for using large puppets
- the *Dossie and Kwame* trilogy

**www.educationalpublications.com.**
**Tel: 0121 344 3004.**

# Early Vision

It isn't always possible to take children out into the wider environment to watch adults in their place of work. Early Vision DVDs aim to bring the real world into settings with short clips of true examples of the real world. Themes include Police, Pets and Ourselves.

**www.earlyvision.co.uk.**
**Tel: 01989 567 353.**

## Puppets by Post

Puppets by Post supply a wide range of innovative hand and finger puppets.
**www.thepuppetcompany.com.**
**Tel: 01462 446 040.**

## 2 Simple

A wide range of software for the foundation stage.
**www.2simple.com.**
**Tel:0800 1072 702.**

## Gymnastics Enterprises

The Funkit bag has been designed to help young children enjoy physical exercise.
**www.earlyyearsfundamentals.co.uk.**
**Tel: 0845 129 7129.**

## Clever Clogs Games

Foundation Steps materials provide open-ended situations that encourage speaking and listening skills and opportunities for early reasoning and problem solving. Three packs are available for the foundation stage – *Three Little Pig Tales, Just Like Me* and *Story Steps*.
**www.cleverclogsgames.co.uk.**
**Tel: 01823 327836.**

## Early Excellence

A wide range of exciting resources designed to support exploratory, role and imaginative play. There is also high quality wooden furniture and storage.
**www.earlyexcellence.com.**
Tel: 01422 311314.